RELIGION AND LIFE IN THE
EARLY VICTORIAN AGE

RELIGION AND LIFE
IN THE
EARLY VICTORIAN AGE

BY
E. E. KELLETT, M.A.

THE EPWORTH PRESS
(EDGAR C. BARTON)
25/35 CITY ROAD, LONDON, E.C.1

CONTENTS

5

INTRODUCTION

IN THIS BOOK I am trying to give my readers some
idea of the religious life of people during one of the
most important half-centuries in all history. But
here I am at once faced with a difficulty. Who
knows even his own little circle in his own little time?
One gathers a few deceptive hints here and there;
one's friends tell him, more or less exactly, their
thoughts, and he translates their words, more or
less correctly, into his own phrases: he may, and
indeed, often must, distort them. As for the notions
of others not his friends, the newspapers pick out
some of them, mainly such as will make good
'copy', and omit the rest. Novels and other books
give what the authors wish to be regarded as their
thoughts, but by no means always what they really
think; nor do they always themselves know what
they think. Out of this confused and cloudy mass
it is impossible to obtain a clear and ordered
conception of what is going on in people's minds.

And the uncertainty is aggravated when we come
to deal with times before our own, as to which our
knowledge is entirely second-hand. Two historians,
writing of the Civil Wars, will give two opposing
accounts, and a third will contrive to give an
account miraculously opposite to both. Here I

always remember the profound words of Froude, 'To be entirely just in our estimate of other ages is not difficult—it is impossible'.

Of these 'other ages' probably the hardest to judge is the one just before our own; we are at once too near it, and too far off. With distant times we may, conceivably, get rid of some of our prejudices; we can discuss the Pharaohs with some measure of impartiality. But our fathers and grandfathers we cannot view 'objectively'—we have known them, loved them, or rebelled against them. Hence the strange caricatures of the Victorian Age drawn by Georgians, which to the survivors of the Victorian Age seem more like sketches of the reign of Nebuchadnezzar than pictures of the time they remember. Similarly, Carlyle and his contemporaries never ceased to exclaim, 'Well, we have *one* thing to rejoice over—we are out of the eighteenth century'. To-day, we are by no means so sure that the eighteenth century was so bad as all that.

I am writing, in the first instance, of the 1830's; and these supply a remarkable illustration of what I have been saying. From early youth I have been familiar with the story of the Oxford Movement. Occasionally I met men who were in the thick of it; and I constantly heard horrified talk of the vagaries of its leaders. On our shelves were many books by Puseyites and many denouncing Puseyism; and I have read perhaps two score of these works. As you study these tomes, varying in literary merit, of every possible shade of opinion, you note one thing in which they all agree, and that is that the Movement convulsed Oxford as if it had been a Lisbon earthquake; that people spoke of nothing else, thought of nothing else, dreamed of nothing else. Crowds thronged to hear Newman at St. Mary's, hung on his lightest words, and listened intent to his very silences. A new *Tract for the Times* comes out, and the booksellers are besieged for copies of it as if it were a Dickens novel. Undergraduates argue about Apostolic Succession as to-day they argue about the merits of cricketers or the chances of the Boat Race. The Latitudinarian Hampden is made Regius Professor by that careless Gallio, Lord Melbourne, and the city resounds as Ephesus resounded when the men cried 'Great is Diana of the Ephesians'. The very scouts take sides and almost come to blows, and the tumult spreads from Common Room to kitchen, while insult after insult is hurled at the unhappy Professor by the raging Tractarians. The noise of battle hurtles in the air, and is heard as far as Rugby, where Dr. Arnold sits down and writes a furious article on 'The Oxford Malignants' to the *Edinburgh Review*. You can almost hear the Newmanites grinding their teeth in answering fury as they read the flaming 'libel'. But the time comes for revenge. Pusey preaches a sermon on Baptismal Regeneration; the anti-Tractarians attack it as if it were a

standard of rebellion, and the Heads of Houses
condemn it without allowing Pusey to say a word in
its defence: the frenzy is renewed, and there is no
Ephesian Town-clerk to soothe the raging multitudes. Then comes the day for the vote to be taken
on Ward's wild and whirling *Ideal of a Christian
Church.* The whole University is there, after a sleep-
less night, to vote, to cheer, to groan; and the Town
watches open-mouthed. Freshmen howl 'Credo in
Newmannum', and dons pass one another with
lowering looks. Bishops draw up their censures
of Tract 90, and two die, perhaps of excitement,
perhaps by the hand of God, before they can deliver
them. Finally, we see Newman retiring to Little-
more, followed by the lamentations of his devotees
and by roars of obloquy from his foes. He seeks
refuge in the Roman Church: some men literally
weep; Gladstone staggers at the news like a drunken
man; others cry gloatingly 'I told you so'.

Now I have on my shelves not only Mozley's
Reminiscences and a dozen other works which tell
you this thrilling tale and give you this unforgettable
impression. I have also a book of *Oxford Memories*
by James Pycroft, dealing with the University at
precisely this time of theological controversy and
religious rancour. Pycroft was at Trinity, Newman's
own original college, at the very moment when
Keble preached the Assize Sermon, in 1833, which
began the great Movement. He was there when, if
one is to believe Froude, Mozley, Church, and the

rest, Newman could not walk a yard out of Oriel but men cried 'Hic est' or 'There he is', and studied his face to read strange matters in it; yet, for all we can gather from two thickish volumes, Pycroft never saw Newman, never heard him, thought nothing of him. He mentions him perhaps twice, to remark that he must not be confused with Dr. Newman of Magdalen, who, strangely enough had the same initials; and it is plain that he held a higher opinion of the Magdalen divine—a genial and easy-going man of the world—than of the ascetic Cardinal to-be. He knew the famous Isaac Williams, who was a Fellow of his College; but he merely says that Williams was too good for this world, and too severe a disciplinarian. While Richard Hurrell Froude was mawkishly hoping that the Oriel undergraduates were observing how regularly he attended chapel, while the leader of the Tractarians was teaching adoring pupils the new-old doctrines, the men Pycroft knew were flirting with shop-girls, stealthily slipping out of college by night and climbing acrobatically back over the railings to avoid discovery; they were running into debt, to the extent of hundreds of pounds, at their tailors'; they were, in their saner moments, hunting, cricketing, rowing, 'shinning up' lamp-posts for wagers. Of the passionate enthusiasm for religion and theology, which fills the pages of other writers, there is not a trace. As for the 'Schools', anxiety about which occupied as

much of the Tractarian minds as could be spared
from controversy on the Apostolic Succession, these
men thought as much of them as did Mr. Verdant
Green's lively friend, Mr. Bouncer. Sufficient unto
the day was the evil thereof: University life was
for enjoyment, and the necessity of passing an
examination at the end of it was a nuisance which
must not be allowed to mar the pleasure. Thus,
whereas Arthur Clough, most distinguished of all
Arnold's Rugby pupils, and most highly-reputed
undergraduate of his day, was so much disturbed
and fretted by the Movement that, to the great
indignation of his old master, he missed his first
class, men of very different intellectual calibre,
paying no heed to theological quarrels, were quite
content if, by the help of a skilful crammer, they
could contrive to gain a Pass degree. For this sole
purpose they would laboriously learn by heart those
Articles of Religion on which Newman was exerting
his subtlest powers of sophistry—and the day after
the examination they forgot them all. While the
morbid Pusey, Professor of Hebrew though he was,
was turning his soul inside out to discover almost
invisible sins, in order to 'confess' them to Keble,
and while he was himself hearing the confessions of
others, the main body of Oxford men, as Pycroft
knew them, were doing what they ought not to
have done, and leaving undone what they ought to
have done, with perfect irresponsibility. Their sins
were certainly greater than any of Pusey's, and were

of the kind which seriously depleted their fathers' purses; but they saw no reason why they should confess them—for the simple reason that everybody knew of them.

Oxford was a small world, of about eight hundred so-called students and a limited number of dons. If, then, two such different pictures can be drawn, by actual observers, of so tiny a society, what must be the feeling of one who tries to give a view of a society not of hundreds but of tens of thousands? You could walk from end to end of the 'city of dreaming spires' in ten minutes, and every member of the University was, at least in theory, an adherent of one denomination. Yet Pycroft was blind to one half of it, Mozley to the other. The people I knew best in my youth were the Methodists, and they were perhaps two millions. I knew them in a dozen different towns, and their character differed according to their municipality. I had also some acquaintance with the country Methodist: he was not very like his town brother. But besides all this, I came across, in various ways, many Nonconformists, and many Church of England people, some High, some Low, some Broad, every one of them with his special idiosyncrasy. If, *mirabile dictu*, some one else had known exactly the same people as I, his account would be no more like mine than Pycroft's is like Mozley's: and, even in the smallest hamlet, no two persons have the same acquaintances.

Again, it is a truism that everybody sees what interests him and passes over what he does not care for. Theodore Hook could repeat the names of all the shopkeepers in almost every street he passed along; a doctor I knew would tell you, at the end of a walk, the diseases he suspected to be carried about by the people he had met. A pretty girl— yes, phthisis; an aldermanic gentleman—dropsy. To the detective, London is a hotbed of criminals; and Sherlock Holmes does not notice the signs of sanctity. And we all tend to imagine that the world is interested, or at least ought to be interested, in the things that interest us. There is a well-known story of a Senior Wrangler who stood up and bowed in the theatre when Queen Victoria was being cheered; and there is another, less well-known, but equally to the point, of a chess-champion who, when he announced his name on ship-board, was astonished to find that no one had ever heard it. When Thiers, the great President of the French Republic, who had guided his country through the terrible years that followed the disaster of 1870, went back to his native town, he met one of the closest friends of his youth. The man recognized him by his face, but by nothing else, and asked him how he had been getting on since they parted.

A story once told me by an American friend of mine struck me forcibly. He lived in a large city, close to a square or circus. In that square were trees—and birds; and he recognized, among these birds, perhaps half a dozen different species. An ornithologist came to stay with him, and stayed in the square instead: in fact he could hardly be dragged from it. After a week of watching and listening, the ornithologist told his host that he had counted two hundred and fifty species, the largest number he had ever come across in so small a space. This is an allegory of the lives of us all.

In describing what I have seen, therefore, I shall be describing only what has been sufficiently interesting to me for me to see it: and in describing times known to me from books or hearsay, I shall be telling only what, in books or in hearsay, has been attractive enough to engage my attention. I begin with the second quarter of the century— a period beyond the memory of any now living. Out of the records my mind makes its own selection —who can say that the selection is representative?

This being my preliminary caution to the reader, I will give, to the best of my ability, what I conceive to have been the main features of the religious life of Evangelical people during the fifty years between 1830 and 1880; years of transition, in which, as I think, more rapid and decisive changes, both in ways of thought and in externals, were wrought than in almost any other half-century of which we have record.

CHAPTER I

THE SOCIAL BACKGROUND

I am not depreciating the divine element in religion
when I say that its manifestations depend on the
social and political environment in which they
appear. Religion, like the Sabbath, is made *for*
man, and it is also made *by* man: and, though it
may remain essentially the same, it will constantly
be changing as men change. If it cannot adapt
itself to its surroundings, it will sooner or later
decay and die. Many instances will occur to the
reader in illustration of this rule. The Roman
Empire, I suppose, had hundreds of different
religions: these gradually gave way, under the
unifying influence of Rome, to the worship of the
Emperor as the symbol of that unity, and finally to
a Christianity which, when the Emperor adopted
the new creed, found itself able to accept him as in
a sense its supreme head on earth, while at the same
time assimilating Greek culture and philosophy.
The chief rival of Christianity, Mithraism, failed
because, though welcomed by the soldiery, it could
not assimilate that culture. It has been noticed how
the monuments of Mithraism, immensely widespread as they are, are not to be found in regions

where Greek influence was strong. Nor is it to be
forgotten that, whereas Christianity found room for
the quiet force of women, Mithraism neglected that
force, and therefore perished.

Similarly, amid difference, with Mohammedanism: it prevailed miraculously in countries twenty or
thirty degrees above and below the Equator, but
no further. Christianity, on the other hand, finds its
strength in its ability to adapt itself to the needs and
characters of very various peoples, and reveals
itself in sundry times and divers manners. But it
cannot do this without itself suffering change. If it
ever conquers the Far East, it will be Oriental;
hitherto it has been Western, and even in the West
it has had many different forms. It has been made
a reproach to Christianity that it is always changing
its aspect, and that its leaders in one age or country
would hardly recognize it if they could see it in
another: but this, despite the quarrels and even
wars to which these differences have given rise, may
be in truth rather a glory than a dishonour. The
Father's house has many mansions.

There were innumerable causes of the Reformation; but one main cause certainly is that, as a new
culture penetrated the Northern Kingdoms, the old
Papalist system was found to be unsuited to them.
And those historians are right who see in the growth
of wealth and trade one secret of the strength of the
anti-Episcopacy of the Caroline times. The House
of Commons in the Long Parliament was three times

as rich as the House of Lords, and inevitably tried therefore to assert its power. Presbyterianism, said Charles II, was no 'religion for a gentleman'; and this was in a sense true: it was the religion of the rising middle classes, and not that of the country nobles and squires on whom the Crown mainly depended. This is no censure on it, though some historians have made it a ground of somewhat virulent denunciation. They seek the causes of the rise of Puritanism in the increasing strength of Mammon, and dilate on the inconsistency between the pretensions of the 'Saints' and the words of Christ. But the right way of putting the case is different. Men, whose commercial instincts were making themselves felt, but who at the same time were conscious of a higher calling, honestly and sincerely sought for a creed which would satisfy their religious aspirations, and found it, according to their varying dispositions, in Presbyterianism, Independency, or some other 'sectarian' form. Circumstances, and natural causes, forbade their acceptance of Anglicanism, but they could not live without devotion, and these forms of religion gave them a God whom they could worship without embarrassment. In the strength of their belief they went on conquering and to conquer; nor is it easy to find in all history men who overcame more stupendous obstacles, showed a more serene faith, or lived more upright lives. There were, it cannot be denied, hypocrites and worldlings among them;

but in every religious field there are tares, and
human limitations are to be found in the holiest of
men.

If the reader has been able to follow this perhaps
dull dissertation, he may be prepared to apply its
conclusions to the Methodism of a hundred years
ago. If he can cast his glances back to that time,
he will see an England astoundingly different,
both politically and socially, from the England
of to-day. As Disraeli put it, very mildly, there
were two nations in our island, the rich and
the poor, and the rich ruled. It was the business
of the poor to submit: if they refused, they were
crushed without mercy. In theory, combinations
of the workers were just possible; in practice they
were suppressed with violence and fraud, though
the masters were allowed to combine as they wished.
The slightest attempt to improve the condition of the
poor was regarded as rebellion, and the law courts,
so far from being a defence against tyranny, were
its bulwark. In the country districts a wage of
eight shillings a week was considered ample; in
the town, the 'truck-system' and other cunning
devices entangled the worker in an inextricable net
of regulations, all of which tended to break his
spirit and debilitate his body. Let me quote here
a summary of the Bolton Report of 1842. 'Anything
like the squalid misery, the slow, mouldering,
putrefying death by which the weak and feeble
of the working classes are perishing here, it never

befell eyes to behold nor imagination to conceive. And the creatures seem to have no idea of resisting or even repining. They sit down with Oriental submission, as if it were God and not the landlord that was laying his hand upon them.' At the same time 'the new Boards of Guardians throughout the country were employing forty or fifty thousand adult men in oakum-picking, stone-breaking, and bone-crushing, in labour-yards attached to the hated "Bastilles of the Poor", on pittances of poor-relief just sufficient to keep their families alive. Men, women, and children, pent up in a dusty atmosphere from five in the morning till seven at night, without change, without intermission, from week to week, fled to the beer-shops on Saturday nights to forget their misery. In such towns few of the labouring classes lived to be thirty: you might occasionally see tottering and broken men and women, grey-haired and aged, whom you took to be eighty, but who were in fact thirty-five or forty'. These were the days when children of six were harnessed to barrows, and driven on with the whip, for eleven hours a day. Out of conditions like this, mill-owners made their tens of thousands a year. These were the days when, as readers of Kingsley know, tiny boys were made to climb chimneys, and constantly died of suffocation, none caring.

In the country districts, as J. L. Hammond has shown, the 'Village Labourer' had to face a lot no more cheerful, save that it was, in certain cases, mitigated by the degrading processes of private charity: an insurance paid by the squires and magistrates to provide against possible revolution. The comfortable classes lived in a state of half-conscious terror; hence these sops to Cerberus, and hence the savagery of their repressions of every overt sign of discontent. We wonder to-day, as we read of the frightful punishments meted out to the 'Captain Swing' agitators, to the 'Blanketeers', to the Tolpuddle Martyrs, or to the Chartists, for what were after all but mild revolts against intolerable conditions; but these horrors were the natural results of fear working on uneasy consciences.

Another form of what to-day would be called 'dope' was religion, artificially administered as a soporific. Not that the rulers themselves believed in it. That was an age which, according to John Stuart Mill, was 'destitute of faith, but terrified at scepticism'—especially the scepticism of the ruled; and Mill tells us that the world would have been amazed to hear how many of its leading men were, and were known by their friends to be, utter unbelievers. Macaulay, with his usual 'heightened and telling' hyperbole, informed the Wilberforces that there were not two hundred men in London who believed in the Bible. But it was desirable that the multitudes should believe in it: and one of the schemes of Castlereagh and Sidmouth, for the purpose of soothing the discontented, was to spend a million pounds on church-building in the dangerous districts. It was recalled that the French Revolution, that bugbear of our statesmen, had been preceded by an outburst of infidelity, and that men so different as David Hume and the High Anglican, William Cole, had been amazed and shocked to find themselves, on their visits to France, in company with people who openly jeered at religion. Within a few years, the Revolution had broken out, and the goddess of Reason had been enthroned in Paris. A dose of quiet, unenthusiastic Christianity could do no harm and might do good : the clergy must preach submission and order, and must inculcate in the poor contentment with the station in which it had pleased God to place them.

The clergy, realizing that they were a department of State, accepted, with due placidity, the task laid upon them. It was a strange position. They were, so to speak, to be fiery advocates of lukewarmness. No better description of the average parson of the time could be given than Froude's account of his father, the Devonshire archdeacon, one of the best specimens of the class, and a man of whom his son, to the end of his life, highly approved. 'In his younger days he had been a hard rider across country. His children knew him as a continually busy, useful man of the world, a learned and cultivated antiquary, and an accomplished artist. Our spiritual lessons did not go beyond the Catechism. About doctrine, Evangelical or Catholic, I do not think that in my early boyhood I ever heard a single word, in church or out of it. Doctrinal controversies were sleeping. People went to church because they liked it, because they knew that they ought to go, and because it was the custom. They had received the Creeds from their fathers, and doubts about them had never crossed their minds.'

This was a legacy from the eighteenth century, with the modifications due to the political and social changes of the intervening years. The scepticism of the ruling classes had been perceived by Bishop Butler as early as 1736: 'it is come, I know not how, to be taken for granted by many persons that Christianity is not so much as a subject of inquiry; but that it is now, at length, discovered to be fictitious.' And yet, though himself a believer, and a defender of the faith, he preached a religion without vitality, and argued for its claims against its opponents as if they were an affair of balanced probabilities. On the whole, he held, the chances in its favour were perhaps six to four, and 'probability was the guide of life'; therefore a prudent man would act as if it were true. On the same principle he told Wesley that his unflinching beliefs and forceful ways were a very terrible thing. Such Christianity was hardly to be distinguished from a reasonable respectability. Bishop Lavington rebuked Wesley on almost exactly the same grounds as those on which the Sadducees rebuked Peter and Paul; he was pretending to certainty where there was none, and exciting the common people when he ought to have been calming them.

Even when, in the 'thirties', a revival of religion took place, it is noteworthy that social evils were largely neglected. Newman, for instance, positively disliked to be reminded that the problems of poverty existed. His idolater, Mozley, tells one or two anecdotes which reveal a very unpleasant insensibility. And one of the very few words of truth in Lytton Strachey's libel on Dr. Arnold of Rugby is to the effect that Arnold's sympathy with the poor was limited to those who were 'good'—that is, submissive and patient. A more genuine Christian than Simeon of Cambridge never lived; but even he dwelt too much on the text that 'the poor we have always with us', concluding that we must make no over-vigorous effort to diminish either their numbers or their poverty.

There was thus, in many parts of the country, and in many strata of society, a determination to keep things as they were, or at any rate to make reforms with a deliberation and a caution hardly to be distinguished from inertia; to suppress impatient people, and to use all possible means for maintaining quiet and keeping peace in that time. The Reform Bill of 1832 excited great hopes; when it became an Act, it was seen to be a Conservative measure, and a deep resentment stirred the minds of those who had been led to expect too much. What it did was merely to give political power to those who already had the power of wealth, and for the poor it did nothing: nay, the little finger of the Whigs was found to be thicker than the loins of Toryism. It was the succeeding forty years which the historian Lecky, contemplating from his easy chair the prosperity of the upper middle-classes, thought the happiest in history. In these same years Karl Marx, studying avidly the miseries of the poor, could see nothing but oppression, tyranny, and 'exploitation of the masses': to him the era was the worst ever known, and there were thousands who agreed with him.

This was the society in which Methodism, during its third and fourth generations, had to live and have its being: and the character and fortunes of that society fashioned the character and fortunes of the Methodists, but in a very peculiar and remarkable manner. It had begun as the religion, in the main, of the lower classes, and Wesley's underlying ideas were, primarily, to 'save poor souls out of the fire' of sin in this world and of hell in the next, and only secondarily to drag them out of the degradation and squalor of their surroundings. At the same time he endeavoured to keep them, or rather to make them, contented citizens of the community, satisfied with their position in life, and trusting in the next world to make up for the inequalities of the present. He would shake the Kingswood colliers out of their bestial indifference in the midst of filth, vice, and irreligion; but he discouraged the very

idea of *political* efforts to improve their status. Like
General Booth in his earlier days, he held that it was
enough for them to seek first the kingdom of God
and his righteousness; the rest would follow, or if it
did not follow, the will of God must be quietly
accepted. He was remarkably successful. Methodism was almost entirely unaffected by Revolutionary
doctrines; the 'Friends of the People' could make
nothing of them; and, amid the disturbances which
followed the conclusion of the Napoleonic War, the
reactionary Tory Government could always rely
on the Methodists to use their influence on behalf of
obedience to the most tyrannical regulations. Not
a single Methodist, so far as I know, took part in
Peterloo; and the Methodist leaders agreed with
Evangelical Churchmen like Wilberforce and
Zachary Macaulay that Sidmouth and Castlereagh
must be supported even in their severest repressive
measures.

Disraeli's division of the people into Two Nations
I have already mentioned. He might, I think, have
gone further, and, like Henry V, as advised by
Archbishop Chichele, have 'divided England into
four'. There was still a vast distinction between the
country and the town, and the country was still of
immense importance. Here there were the county
gentry and the village poor. In the towns were, on
the one hand, the wealthy manufacturers and the
well-to-do shopkeepers, and on the other the poor
and downtrodden workers. But the poor townsfolk

differed from the poor villagers. Despite all the
frightful difficulties of which I have spoken, it was
just possible, in certain cases, for the artisan to rise
into the ranks of the well-to-do, or even into the
ranks of the rich masters and employers. The system
of Napoleon dropped the theory of liberty and
equality, substituting for it that of 'la carrière
ouverte aux talents'. Every soldier had a marshal's
baton in his knapsack. The same doctrine prevailed
in the Britain of Victorian days. With thrift, energy,
and good fortune the poorest might become rich—
and some did. Thus, while Methodism began as the
religion of the masses, it was constantly finding that
some of the masses were lifting themselves above
their fellows. Even in Wesley's days this was the
case, and inevitably so; for, as he remarked again
and again, religion meant sobriety and thrift,
and sobriety and thrift meant wealth. But did
wealth mean an increase, or even a continuance,
of piety? Certainly not always; and Wesley, when
he found that, as the door was opened to Mammon,
religion flew out, dealt drastically with the evil. I
have been told that class-books still exist, showing
how ruthlessly Wesley excluded from his societies
men who, having become rich, had ceased to live as
he conceived Methodists ought to live. He preferred the humble penny a week and shilling a
quarter from the religious poor to the guineas of
insincere opulence. A man who, out of an income
of a hundred and twenty pounds a year, spent only

twenty-eight on himself, and who, at his death, left only ten pounds behind him, was not likely to trouble about the wealth of others. But there were, needless to say, many men who, though rich, contrived to get through the needle's eye of Wesley's rigid inspection, and that without hypocrisy; and there were, doubtless, others who skilfully avoided exclusion though their piety was not what it had been. As time went on, it is true, some, rising in the world, sought social advancement by joining the Church of England, but some, knowing that power and distinction are more easily gained in smaller societies than in larger, remained. Nor was it always necessary to go elsewhere for the sake of prestige. In many places Methodism and Non-conformity received the respect of the highest circles. In Leeds, to take one example, the 'best people' from the 'thirties' to the 'sixties', were Methodists.

Not forgetting, however, that human motives are mixed, and that even in the earliest days of Christianity it was impossible to secure an absolutely untainted Church, I can say with confidence that Methodism need fear no fair comparison with other religious societies. Though it is invariably the case that in the third or fourth generation of a movement which has succeeded, there is great danger of a decline in sincerity and fervour, Methodism wonderfully surmounted its difficulties. The histories of the denomination, and the biographies of its heroes, are full of the names of noble men who, having gained wealth and position, devoted their money and gave their leisure to the service of religion and of their fellow men, regarding their means as a trust to be used not for personal ends but for the Giver. Many such men I personally knew, simple, honest, unspoilt by success, and respected by all whose respect was worth having. That there were men of another stamp is only to be expected; the purse-proud and tyrannical rich we have always with us; but in my considered belief no Church, in proportion to its numbers, has ever had fewer.

At the same time, it was impossible for Methodism long to escape the influence of the Time-Spirit, and the Societies soon showed in miniature the character of the community at large. Methodism gradually became more Nonconformist, and the poorer members, like Nonconformists in general, tended to Radicalism, some few of the ministers leading the way. But the wealthier, whether Conservative or Liberal, had the natural feelings of their class. Thus, when the evils of the Industrial system began to be revealed, when the Bolton Report was published, and when Michael Sadler and Lord Shaftesbury started their agitation for reform, the leading Methodists, like the leading men in other Non-conformist Churches, were found in the ranks of opposition. As Hammond has said, the Church clergy opposed the repeal of the Corn Laws, the Nonconformist, and the Methodist with them, opposed the Ten Hours Bill. The reader will

remember that Shaftesbury never forgave Bright
for his conduct on this occasion; there were many
Methodists he would never have forgiven had he
known their names. As a strong Evangelical he
sympathized with Methodism and in a measure
understood it; he met Methodists in Exeter Hall
and took the chair at Methodist lectures; but he
could not understand why the denomination did not
work whole-heartedly with him in his philanthropic
enterprises. Why did it not perceive that the
factory-owners were trusting in oppression and
becoming vain in robbery? Why could they preach
sermons on the sorrows of the poor and the sighing
of the needy, and yet do nothing to alleviate the
misery?

The fact is that within the small realm of
Methodism there were, as in the larger realm of
England, Disraeli's Two Nations: and there was
between them the same misunderstanding as in the
wider world. We must not blame the rich too
harshly. As John Bright, conscious of his own
rectitude, could not believe that other masters
needed the strong arm of the law, so with many of
these. When Bright was slandered by his Tory foes
as a tyrannical factory-owner, his workers gave him
a testimonial which showed that those who knew
him best trusted him most; and I have known men
of like kind with Bright. Those were the days which
Lord Baldwin has described, when his father knew
every one of his men by their Christian names, and

when the factory was almost a family; when the
head was accessible to all, and was ready to hear of
grievances and where possible to redress them.
What the law insisted on their doing they had done
voluntarily, and much more; and they resented
what they regarded as unnecessary compulsion,
and felt the stigma compulsion seemed to imply.
They were like the better slave-owners of the South,
who knew themselves to be innocent of the crimes
imputed to them by the Abolitionists, who were to
their slaves like Abraham to his servants, and for
whom the slaves, had they been permitted to do so,
would have fought against those who fought to
free them. But masters and slave-owners alike
forgot that the law is for the bad and not for the
good; and in their sympathy with their colleagues
they often refused to admit the truth of charges
against the worse members of their class. Such
members unfortunately there were, and too many of
them.

Thus, in the manufacturing towns, one might see
the wealthier families supporting the Church by
taking the better and more expensive pews at the
back, while the cheaper or free sittings were
occupied by less distinguished people; and there
was real risk of the snobbery denounced by St.
James in his letter to the twelve tribes of the
Dispersion. There may also have been some
ostentation in the gifts made at the collections;
but I do not wish to imply the slightest depreciation

of the generosity almost invariably shown, alike by the rich and by the indigent, in every congregation I have known. The amounts subscribed were indeed astonishing; most men gave far more than the canonical tithe of their incomes, and some, for years in succession, gave a third. John Wesley's injunction, 'Get all you can, save all you can, give all you can', was faithfully obeyed; and I have had Anglican friends who have positively refused to believe that the collections, in chapels holding perhaps half the number of people a church could accommodate, averaged twice or three times as much as those which the clergyman was accustomed to reckon upon. These were for all purposes, horse-hire funds, ministers' widows, retired ministers, local preachers, foreign and home missions, the poor of the congregation, and who knows what; and the givers gave with discrimination, according to the needs of the funds or their sympathy with them. Here the ministers themselves were not behind-hand; some I have known who seriously crippled themselves by too lavish a generosity.

While it was strongly held that to make the poor religious was the best way of relieving their distress—and there is much to be said for this belief—there was a vast amount of work which anticipated the philanthropic labours of more recent times, and which ought not to be forgotten. Some of it was absolutely amazing. In the 'sixties' there was a mission in a central London slum called Chequer

Alley, a haunt of inconceivable squalor, vice, and
crime, which even the police dreaded to visit.
Ministers and laymen, risking health and even life,
entered this purlieu in the spirit of John Hunt or
John Williams carrying Christianity to cannibal
islands.[1] The results were miraculous; in a few
months the place was transformed, drunkenness
almost ceased, harmony reigned instead of per-
petual discord, savage husbands and sullen wives
were reconciled, and Chequer Alley became an
oasis in the desert of London lawlessness and horror.
Nor did the miracle-workers forget more mundane
methods. Remembering Wesley's saying that clean-
liness is next to godliness, they taught the merits of
soap and water, and took care that as much sunshine
as can possibly be found in such an Erebus should
be allowed to penetrate into the dwellings. A calm
and unexaggerated account of this mission was
published by the Rev. Frederick W. Briggs, one of
the ministers concerned. But there were many
others, not less notable, of which no history has
ever been written, unless the Recording Angel has
entered the story in the Book of Life.

In the agricultural districts—then, I repeat,
vastly more important, relatively to the towns, than
now—conditions were different. As a rule, the
squire and his ally the parson still dominated the
place, and it was rarely that the farmer became a

[1] The movement was begun by a noble woman, Miss M'Carthy, whose
name should not be forgotten. Small and insignificant, as I have heard,
in bodily presence, she had the soul of a hero.

Methodist. Thus the little chapel was in most cases occupied by the poor—not many noble, not many of the great in this world were called. Of necessity the services were usually taken by local preachers, the minister appearing perhaps once or twice in the quarter; and the local preachers were drawn from the ranks of the labourers. An example which everybody knows is the Tolpuddle Martyrs, some of whom were local preachers of unblemished character—which did not save them from the most savage penalties. The chapels were in some cases looked on with jealous eyes by the authorities: the squire suspected them as homes of sedition, the parson as nursing-grounds of schism. But this was by no means always the case. Where the parson was of an easy-going temper, he was perfectly willing to tolerate a sectarianism which saved the village constable work, and which did not interfere with Church and State. On the chapel side, also, there was willing co-operation. Down to times within the memory of men still living, Methodists, regarding themselves as in a sense members of the National Church, would attend the parish church in the mornings, listen more or less attentively to the imperfect gospel as preached by the rector, and go in the afternoons or evenings to the chapel to hear the fuller evangel proclaimed by their chosen messenger. An old minister told me that in one of his first circuits he was on the friendliest terms with the clergyman, who frankly informed him that he

regarded him as an inexpensive curate. 'Go on, my
boy,' said he; 'your religion is a little wilder than
mine, but it is essentially the same. Both as rector
and as justice of the peace I appreciate the work you
are doing.'

With the growth of the High Church movement,
and with the spread of Radical feeling, this state of
things became impossible. The clergy came to
regard the Methodists as dangerous rather than
helpful; and the magistrates scented the rise of
subversive opinions. The times were ripening for
Joseph Arch and for the enfranchisement of the
agricultural labourer. A starvation-wage, supple-
mented by charity, was no longer satisfying the
farm-hand. And this point of view was gradually
being appreciated in higher quarters. No longer,
probably, would a judge speak to the country-
people as Baron Alderson spoke in 1831 to the
tenants of Lady Cavan (Dr. Arnold's sister), who
had asked that their wage of nine shillings a week
should be increased. 'You have not been respectful.
If your wages are insufficient, you should trust in
the proved benevolence of your superiors. In no
country does charity fall in a purer stream than in
this. Appeal properly for help, and the appeal
will never be in vain.' He then sentenced the
delinquents to hard labour: and they were fortunate, for many others were sentenced to trans-
portation for life. By the 'seventies', though there
were still horrible cases of poverty and tyranny, the

nation had become enlightened, and it was perceived that what the labourers needed was not charity but justice.

At the same time the flight from the land was increasing in rapidity and in volume. As the position of the town-worker was improving, and as the demand for labour was daily growing, the villages were being inevitably depopulated, until the state of things we see to-day had come in. The squire had fewer tenants and smaller rents, the parson fewer parishioners, the chapel fewer attendants. England woke up to the fact that whereas a hundred years before she could feed herself and even export a little food, now a six-weeks' blockade would mean starvation. The cry 'Back to the Land' was raised, and has so far been raised in vain. Whether, as Dean Inge and others think, the days of the Industrial Revolution are nearly over; whether, in the natural course of events, the towns will again decline, the urban population diminish, and the rural districts once more come by their own; these are questions which only time can answer. Should Dr. Inge be right, we shall, I imagine, see Methodism still in existence, but accommodating itself to new conditions by adopting new devices, not, however, entirely breaking contact with its ancient self.

CHAPTER II

THE MINISTER

I HAVE THOUGHT that perhaps the best way of conveying some idea of the religious conditions of the time I am describing may be to take certain typical 'characters', in the style, if not with the skill, of an Overbury or an Earle, and paint them as distinctly as I can; and the first which occurs to me is naturally—for my father was a Methodist minister—the character whose name heads this chapter. I shall, of course, speak in the main of the minister of this Church; and it will be remembered that he differed in very material points from his Baptist or Congregational brother. In some respects he was more like a Church of England clergyman than a Nonconformist pastor.

One point of difference was that the Methodist minister, despite the stubborn evidence of facts, did not regard himself as a Dissenter, though he would sometimes own that he was a Nonconformist. He held what he regarded as the true Church of England doctrines, while he could not always conform to her external practices. A trace of John Wesley's ideas could still be seen in him; and there were signs that he looked on himself as supplementing rather than opposing the work of the clergyman. There were, as I have said, places where the Methodists went to the church in the morning to hear the imperfect gospel, and to chapel in the afternoon and evening to hear it in its Evangelical fullness. Thus you might often find a friendly feeling between the rector and the minister: and this lasted, in some districts, to the 'fifties'. My father, for example, in a country circuit to which he was appointed in early youth, was effusively welcomed by the rector, and the friendship thus begun was kept up for more than forty years. For a minister, or his son, to pass into the Church was not regarded as apostasy; and in the 'Crockford' of the time you could find many Methodist names, such as Ogilvy, a Fellow of Balliol, mentioned by Mozley, Farrar, afterwards of Durham University, Archdeacon Hannah, Richard Watson Dixon, and others. The feeling then was quite different from what it was later, when the High Church party had gained ground, and when the 'conversion' involved a complete change of attitude. I recall a story told me by an old ex-President. He was on a voyage to Australia, and a certain clergyman was a fellow-traveller. It chanced that the conversation turned on the Methodists, and the clergyman, in a patronizing tone, said that 'as far as he had heard they were often very decent people'. He little knew that among the company was one of the 'decent people', who had recognized him, and knew his history. After letting him run on for some time, the old minister said, with some indignation, 'Well, I am glad you speak well of the Methodists, and have *heard* of them; for you received your theological training in one of their colleges, and you were one of their ministers for several years'. In the early Victorian days, as far as I can discover, the feeling on both sides was different. The seceder was not ashamed of his old friends, and his old friends did not resent the secession.

There was another feature which to-day seems strange. Not for some time did the Temperance question assume the importance which, in my early recollection, it had attained. The evils of intemperance were, of course, seen, but they were not to be extirpated by direct or organized attack; and few ministers were total abstainers. You could still see, in country places, chapels built close to inns, in order that the preacher might refresh himself with the traditional beverage which, it was still maintained, had won Crécy and Agincourt; and I have heard of some who, to strengthen themselves for the sacred warfare, would take the same spirit with which sailors were dosed before secular battles. Those who could afford it were, in what was then thought moderation, drinkers of wine; and hardly any would refuse it when it was offered. It was, I think, in the 'forties' that a cry arose, urging ministers to join the crusade against intemperance, and to set the example of entire abstinence. Several of them resented the attempt to limit their freedom, and Dr. Osborn, in Conference, declared, with his usual force, that he was going to have his glass when he wanted it. In the troubles that followed, the more unscrupulous agitators accused their enemies of excess, and made great capital out of very little. It may have been in self-defence that so many, in the subsequent years, adopted Rechabite principles. It is at any rate certain that men like Dr. Alder would be astonished if asked to dine, as they would be to-day, without anything more intoxicating than lemonade. So great, in fact, is the change that I knew an eminent minister so utterly ignorant of intoxicants as to accept and enjoy a glass of cherry-brandy, which his mischievous host assured him was a temperance drink. 'Really, Mr.——,' said he, 'I never knew there were temperance drinks so nice as this.' In the 'thirties' there were ministers who could not easily have been thus deceived. Some of them were first-class judges of wine, and might, if they had gone to Oxford, have been put, like John Henry Newman, in charge of the college cellar.

But a still greater contrast between old and new could, I believe, be found in a totally different sphere. The attitude of the minister is now much more humble than it was. 'A minister', says a holder of the office to the little heroine of that famous story, *Jessica's First Prayer*, 'is a servant, the servant of God and of man'; and the definition

certainly accords with the derivation of the word.
But the Pope also proclaims himself as 'the servant
of the servants of God', and yet contrives to exert
a very vigorous authority; and I fear that, rightly
or wrongly, my early impressions of a minister were
rather of a master than of a servant. He ruled, and
so far as I could see, he meant to rule. Obedience
was the business of the laity, to give commands the
right and duty of the pastor. He was not, of course,
a believer in the High Church doctrine of the
Apostolic Succession; but, as I heard one of the
order maintain, 'My position is of divine origin,
though I should trace it rather to St. Paul than to
St. Peter. There must be subordination'; and he
proceeded to urge his point in a speech not dis-
similar to that of Ulysses on 'Degree' in 'Troilus and
Cressida'. Others, also, at times, spoke of themselves in a way curiously reminding one of the
claims made by the Puseyites: they magnified their
office, and thought it right to do so. This attitude,
in the not very distant past, had caused serious
difficulties, ending sometimes in open revolts; and
the consequent struggles had not been forgotten.
There had, it is true, been victories, but the victories
were Pyrrhic, and the losses had been heavy; yet
many ministers clung obstinately to the old ideas.
One determined veteran Tory openly said, when the
laity were admitted to Conference in 1878, and a
layman died in the first few days, 'It is a judgement'. Forty or fifty years before that, as far as

one could learn, the feeling was stronger and more widespread; and this was the more remarkable as the whole body had been terror-struck and exasperated by the arrogance of the Tractarian assumptions, and much annoyed by the growing contempt with which they were being treated by the Church of England clergy. Whereas, in the days of Evangelical supremacy, there had been the friendliness between Methodists and the Church which I have described, that friendliness was now impossible. Yet the ministers were often accused by their congregations of behaving to them exactly as the Tractarians behaved to their parishioners: it was 'Popery' in embryo.

This antagonism, strangely crossed with affection as it often was, had been a main cause of the disruptions which, after Wesley's death, had so gravely weakened Methodism both numerically and spiritually. Alexander Kilham had 'gone out' in 1796, and had taken with him a goodly number of the laity. Then had followed the Warrenite secession of the 'thirties', a secession which, though nominally on another point, was really due to the growing sense that the ministerial body was too despotic. Finally, came the terrible explosion of 1849. It is true that the three leaders, Everett, Dunn, and Griffith, had very little true democratic feeling; Dunn, in fact, as everybody knows who has read the *Life of General Booth*, was an autocrat born and bred; but after their expulsion they had to seek support from the democrats, and to pay at least lip-service to democracy; and it was easy for them to represent the Conference which drove them out as very similar to a Venetian oligarchy. Itself, during thirty years, dominated by the will of one masterful man, it had been unflinching in dominating the congregations committed to its charge. Some of the ministers made no attempt, of the kind so often made by tyrants, to disguise their tyranny under Republican forms. In the very midst of the great Disruption, when laymen were leaving in tens of thousands, one superintendent addressed his 'flock' in uncompromising terms. 'Yes,' he said, 'the laity are sheep and the minister the shepherd. Whoever heard of sheep ruled by a sheep? It is your business to go where the shepherd bids.' The sheep, however, not admitting the truth of the analogy, went where they willed, and next Sunday the chapel was all but empty.

Part of this antagonism was due to the fact that in politics the pulpit still retained its old Toryism, while the pew was rapidly growing more Radical. At a General Election Thomas Garland, one of the most highly respected ministers, had the audacity to speak from a Liberal platform: he was gravely censured by Dr. Bunting, who had himself openly supported a Tory candidate. When Garland pointed out this awkward fact, Bunting was not in the least disconcerted. To speak for a Tory was to speak for religion; to defend Liberalism was perilously near to helping the Wicked One. Already Joseph Rayner Stephens had been expelled for his Chartist activities. But the multitude was no longer what it had been. When, at the time of the Peterloo massacre, the Reformers tried to secure Methodist assistance, they found little or none. Why trouble about votes or equality in this world? All evils would be set right in the next; and, to the lasting disgust of men like Bamford (who has vigorously recorded his feelings in his autobiography), the vast power of Methodism was either not used at all or was used on the side of oppression. But that state of things had immensely altered since 1819. The Methodist laity were sympathizing with Dissent in a way which would have surprised John Wesley, and with the Felix Holts and Alton Lockes in a way which, though the ministers only half knew it, made them suspicious. They uneasily sensed a latent rebellion, and, as so often in such cases, asserted their authority all the more violently as it was slipping from them. Just as, in the Conference itself, a whisper was going round that 'Dr. Bunting must not be allowed to have things all his own way', so in the Church at large it was being muttered that the ministry must be, gently but firmly, restrained: and in both cases the struggles of the despot to keep power increased the determination that the power should be diminished.

Some idea of the bitterness with which these early battles were carried on may be gained from the peculiar literature which it produced. Not Martin Marprelate himself was more libellous than the author of *The Round Preacher*, which appeared just after the Warrenite agitation, and which was written by a minister who seceded and entered the Church of England. According to this writer, every Wesleyan minister was a compound of despotism, tempered by his slavery to a still more despotic wife, and the most nauseating hypocrisy. Pretending to have set his affections solely on things above, he was in reality a miser, a glutton, and an unscrupulous grasper after worldly power. The violence of the slander is such as to overreach itself; and the impression one gains after reading it is that the Church of England had no reason to be proud of a recruit capable of so venomous a series of falsehoods; but there is, I think, a grain of truth at the bottom. There was a certain arrogance in the ministerial body of which it was quite unconscious, but which roused just resentment: and when the opportunity arose, that resentment overflowed, and expressed itself in exaggerated forms. I might compare it with the outbreak of the French Revolution. The grievances which caused the Revolution were real; but, when once the feelings they stirred were released, they rushed forward in a torrent, and men both said and did far more than they really meant. So it was in 1789; and so it was in the smaller upheavals of 1830 and 1849.

Fortunately, in calmer times, there were mitigating circumstances which kept things within bounds. Many ministers, of course, were humble, modest, and so genuinely saintly that, on the one hand, they never presumed, and, on the other, the laity were willing to concede them more than they desired. They ruled without knowing it, and made their way by the irresistible force of sheer goodness. There were also many laymen who bore in mind the Pauline maxim not to think of themselves more highly than they ought to think: honest, true, not slothful in business, serving the Lord. There were others who took the whole thing in a humorous spirit, smiling quietly at what they regarded as assumption, but not thinking it worth making a fuss about. 'Let the minister lecture us in the pulpit,' said yet others of a slightly different cast of mind; 'but so long as he doesn't interfere with me in the shop, I shan't worry. After all, if he carries things too far, we can always refuse to invite him at the end of each year, and at the end of three he automatically goes.' On the whole, then, there was harmony: the congregations rendered unto God the things that were God's, and for the rest treated themselves as Cæsars, and rendered unto Cæsar often in too rich a measure, the things that were his. And, in those congregations, there were nearly always some who loved their minister, when he was worthy of it, with a discriminating yet passionate affection, and parted from him, when the time came, with unaffected grief.

Many illustrations, amusing or otherwise, of what I have been saying, could easily be given: some from tradition, others from written records. If the ordinary minister was, in his own domain, a ruler, the President was a ruler *in excelsis*. I have heard stories from old men of the way in which they had, in Conference, been suppressed by the chair. 'Sit down, brother,' said the President, in tones the reverse of fraternal, when they rose to points of order: and I have been told that no less a man than Henry Moore, unused to contradiction, told a man who disagreed with him that 'what he was saying was as false as hell'. Much later than Moore's time, a certain President visited Kingswood School during his year of office. He unceremoniously took charge of affairs, deposed, for the time being, the Head, and conducted the short morning service in his own fashion. The Head ought certainly to have imitated Dr. Goodall of Eton, who, when Royalty visited the school, did not remove his cap, in order that the boys might remain unaware that there was in the country a greater man than the Head Master. Not so the Kingswood magnate. He was taken completely by surprise, and meekly yielded place. The President announced the hymn, and—as was the custom then and for many years afterwards— read out each verse. As he was reading one of the verses, he noticed that one of the lads seemed inattentive. He paused; and in the commanding voice which had awed the boys' fathers a week or two before, thundered out, 'If that boy will only look at *Me*—

> 'And gaze, transported at the sight,
> To all eternity.'

The same sense of indisputable mastership was shown, in its measure, through all the grades of the hierarchy. I was told, many years after the occurrence of the incident, by the son of a Superintendent minister, how his father had been at once bewildered and filled with righteous indignation when he met with opposition at the Quarterly Meeting. Who was Mr. Jones, a layman though a local-preacher, to venture to cross his appointed spiritual guide? 'But,' he said to his wife when he reached home, accepted the slippers which his dutiful helpmeet had warmed for him, and sank into his chair to enjoy the clay pipe which he regularly smoked before retiring, 'but, my dear, I gave him at least as good as I got.' It is to be feared that though he resented the impertinence of Mr. Jones, he savoured the zest of battle; he had the 'stern joy which warriors feel in foemen worthy of their steel'. More sensitive men, to use their own phrase, were 'not angry but grieved' on such occasions; it saddened them that there were so many stubborn people who would not recognize legitimate authority.

As time went on, the laity availed themselves more and more fully of their freedom, and the ministers meekly submitted. I was present once at

D

a meeting in which the minister was plainly told
that his sermons were too long and too metaphysical.
Fortunately, he was of a placid and humorous
disposition. He answered that he knew his defects,
and was anxious to improve. He would therefore
place his pulpit at the service of his critic, and try
to learn how to preach from an example which,
to judge from the eloquence of the denunciation he
had just heard, was certain to be an admirable
one. Here was the soft answer which turneth away
wrath. Another minister, on his arrival in a
circuit, and at the very reception-meeting which is
supposed to be specially impregnated with benevolence, was told to be careful not to interfere too
much. 'You know nothing of this place, and we
would have you remember that you are on your trial.'
He answered that he hoped the trial would be a
fair one, and prayed that the jury would be merciful.
I am happy to say that no superintendent I ever
knew was more greatly beloved by his circuit than
this minister, who, though no compelling orator,
was a tireless visitor and a tactful member of the
society.

A means which was sometimes used for conveying
a hint to the minister was the prayer meeting.
After a very eloquent discourse in a Yorkshire
pulpit, an old local preacher, who imagined that
the minister needed a little friendly admonition,
took his opportunity with both hands. 'Lord, bless
our minister. Tha knaws he can preach, but,

Lord, keep him 'umble.' A loud 'Amen' from the victim of this supplication showed that the shaft had gone home. Sometimes the attack was a little less amicable. A minister's wife was regarded as too worldly: she had an income of her own, and dressed too well. It was held that her husband ought to have checked this extravagance, and the prayer-meeting was here also utilized for the purpose of conveying to him the prevailing sentiment. As, by a kind of 'judgement' for this ostentation, the lady suffered from rheumatism, and never knelt at prayers, there was a second cause of offence. But both she and her husband were a little vexed when she heard divine aid called upon to punish her. 'Lord', cried a man well-known for his power of mixing metaphors, 'melt the stubborn knees, melt them from their seats. And save us from the pride of silks and satins; let our ornament be a meek and quiet spirit.'

The minister's wife, of course, might be a very important personage: if she was sociable, tactful and natural, the situation was often vastly eased. Good temper was essential; and in this connexion I often think of the sound advice given by Adam Clarke in his 'Letter to a Junior Methodist Preacher'. Clarke was an astonishing scholar, but also a man of worldly wisdom. In this letter he not only advises the young man as to brushing his teeth with water, avoiding all deleterious powders, but adds precepts as to his matrimonial adventures.

'Choose as your wife', he says, 'a woman of natural good temper apart from grace, so that if she falls from grace you may still have an endurable married life.' Incidentally, I may remark that even in this practical counsel there is a dash of controversial theology. For Clarke's early youth had been passed in the thick of the Antinomian strife. He remembered Toplady's savage attacks on Wesley's 'rotten Arminianism', and was steeped in Fletcher's 'Checks'. A main doctrine of Antinomianism is that a fall from grace is impossible. Thus, while giving his pupil directions as to his way of life, the great commentator insinuates a warning against heresy.

How the young preacher was to detect the difference between serenity born and serenity acquired, even Clarke was apparently unable to inform him : but it was certainly desirable that a minister's wife should possess the quality whatever its origin. She needed it; and very often, as I have heard and seen, used it to good effect. A story I once read, evidently a transcript from the life, embodied a long conversation between the minister's wife and the wives of a dozen laymen. These women, at first somewhat antagonistic to their pastor, are in the end completely won over; and we are left to hope that they will exert their irresistible influence, in their turn, over their husbands. That discord which, as the poet says, is harmony misunderstood, would soon be resolved, and a blessed peace would reign.

Unluckily, not all wives had the chance of performing such miracles. Ministers' families in the Victorian age were large—as indeed were most families—and the mother had usually quite enough to do with looking after her children without playing the part of her husband's second in command. It might well happen that two children came in the course of the regulation three years' sojourn in a circuit; where was leisure to be found and where was the place for Church-work? Too frequently the mother was worn out before her time, and if she did not die prematurely was more or less of a wreck. The management of a household, the careful attention to every penny of expenditure, and worries of all kinds, made one wonder how she found time for attendance at the chapel and at the class-meeting, to say nothing of social duties.

By the time when my own memory begins to function, I think the character of the ministers, and their relations with the laity, were undergoing a change. Whether this was actually the case, or whether I happened to fall among men, on both sides, of equable and sensible dispositions, the fact remains that it would not be easy to find more delightfully harmonious societies than many of the circuits in which I spent my time. Friendly feeling, obviously perfectly unforced, showed itself on all occasions; and the inevitable result was a smooth and increasing success in the Christian work of the Church. Humour and goodwill found out the way.

Many, but of course by no means all, of the ministers I knew were indefatigable readers; some real scholars. The hours from nine to one were rigidly, by large numbers, set aside for study or for the preparation of sermons: and here the Methodists had a great advantage over Congregationalists or others who were confined to a single church. One sermon would do for several congregations, and the terrible wear and tear of producing two new ones every week was avoided. Not that the sermon remained the same. A diligent preacher revised it, improved it, and sometimes completely rejuvenated it. Since very few preachers, like Dr. Punshon, recited *memoriter*, or, like Dr. Dallinger, read their sermons from manuscript, the mere change of audience might leave the 'three parts and conclusion' unaltered, but vitally metamorphosed everything else. As Demosthenes said, the audience makes the speaker; and I have seen the 'same' sermon fall a little flat with a stolid congregation, and, being delivered with fire and energy to another, make a strong impression. To use a phrase then common, the preacher had 'had liberty', because he had felt sympathy in his hearers. On one occasion, I heard a minister, whose records had gone wrong, preach the same sermon within three weeks from the same pulpit; but such was the freshness of his treatment, due perhaps to his better health or spirits, that his hearers, as I discovered afterwards, had no notion that they had heard it before.

The three-year system added to this advantage. A change of environment made it possible— provided the minister was not a mere lazy self-repeater—to gar the auld discourses look maist as guid as new. And, as men of force and originality are not numerous, it seems to me that this system, so much decried, is on the whole the best. I recall cases which, I think, indicate this from the negative point of view. An excellent Congregational minister of my acquaintance, of average ability, was more than acceptable to his people for three years, and, had he left then, would have been remembered with affection and admiration. By the end of the fourth, he had exhausted his store of thought, and his people with it. They endured him for another two years with ever-increasing weariness, and then —in pain and irritation on both sides—they parted. It cannot be too often remembered that the great are few, and that legislation should be for those who are 'seated in the mean'.

There is another aspect of the same thing which is worth a moment's notice. Even if the Congregational minister chances to be of the able minority, he has to spend so much time over his sermons that pastoral work becomes impossible, and the people never see him save on formal occasions. My readers can supply their own examples:

I could, if it were worth while, easily give a dozen. On the whole, I think, the people would give their vote for the good pastor and poor preacher as against the eloquent man who never visits.

But, be the cause what it may, many of the Methodist ministers I knew, enjoying thus a morning generally free from interruption, used it to great advantage. Steady and close reading gave them stores of information, if not of technical scholarship, which few Oxford or Cambridge dons could rival. One minister of my acquaintance told me that he had begun by learning his sermons by heart, but found that this habit not only spoilt the freedom of his actual delivery, but was, by the time it took, a serious hindrance to study. He had therefore renounced it, and never regretted his choice. He used to recount an anecdote told by the great French Protestant preacher, Athanase Coquerel. Several pastors had met together to discuss the best method of preaching, and the debate turned on the respective merits of the extempore and the *memoriter*. A devotee of the latter got up, and spoke, on the spur of the moment, so admirably against extemporaneous preaching, demonstrating impromptu his total incapacity to speak impromptu, that all said it was impossible for him to have better refuted himself. 'He did at any rate', said my friend, 'prove that when the mind is full the words will come.' Here he agreed with old Cato the Censor, and with the opinion expressed by Faust to Wagner:

> 'Und wenn's euch ernst ist, was zu sagen,
> Ist's nöthig, Worten nachzujagen?'

It certainly, then, was not always laziness, but a reasoned conviction, that led so many Methodist ministers to content themselves with preparing the substance of their discourses, and leaving the choice of the words to the inspiration of the moment.

The morning's reading or writing thus finished, the minister was restored to his family at lunch-time, and more often than not, brought forth the stores he had been accumulating for the benefit of his children; sometimes, to use the words of Fuller on John Scotus Erigena, 'pouring learning into his lads rather in proportion to the plenty of the fountain than to the receipt of the vessels'. Nevertheless, they often contrived to learn much, and in after days found an unexpected use for what they had learned. To take my own case, it was at table that I first heard that 'Tertullian was a Montanist', that Marcion, though a noble man, was a Gnostic, that the Docetists held peculiar views as to the deity of Christ: unintelligible dicta which took their place in my mind years after-wards.

This interval, lucid or the reverse, was almost the father's only chance of influencing his children; for at breakfast—a hasty meal, agitated for them by

the necessity of rushing off to be in time for school—
he was a ruthless devourer of letters and the
newspaper, and often forgot to eat until the younger
members had been forced to depart. And, from
two or three o'clock onwards, he was, if a conscientious pastor, as diligent in his 'rounds' as a
family doctor. For weeks together, in fact, his
children scarcely saw him except during that one
precious hour; and I sometimes think the people
who complained that the 'sons of the prophets' did
not always live up to their privileges failed to realize
how slight those privileges were. A layman, if so
inclined, might enjoy the company of his family for
some hours every evening; the minister's family
scarcely ever saw their father after sunset; and if,
as often happened, they were sent to boarding-
school, never at all. What increased the number
of these absences was the pressure of all sorts of
committees and other meetings; and here I think
the Methodist ministry was more greatly afflicted
than any other. An eminent Congregational pastor,
whom I knew well, told me that, much as he
appreciated the conversation of his Methodist
friends, he never had a chance of enjoying it to the
full; for as soon as the talk had got well under way,
the Methodist would look at his watch and remark
that he must hurry off to some convention. The
Doctor said he felt like Dr. Johnson, who complained
that, so soon as John Wesley became specially
interesting, he was off. 'This was painful to a

man who likes to fold his legs and have his talk out.'

Realization of these evils led some ministers to give up their Monday mornings, despite the proverbial 'Mondayishness' which all ministers feel, to small social meetings, which their colleagues of various denominations would attend. Though a laic of the laics, I was more than once admitted to these little gatherings, and very interesting they were. For some weeks in two or three successive vacations, I joined two ministerial friends. After half an hour of ordinary talk, the Hebrew Bibles were brought out, and study began. I myself knew the letters and a few of the elements of the grammar; one of the others knew a little more; the third commanded a good vocabulary and had the declensions and conjugations at his finger-ends. I have never ceased to be grateful for the hours thus spent. When we had finished a chapter or two, as often as not a third minister would drop in, and some very pleasant and informative conversation would follow. These men were shrewd, humorous, capable, and also, as no one could deny who saw them in such conditions, serious and diligent Christians.

I do not deny that not all were like them. That very freedom, and that very abundance of leisure, which constrained the conscientious man to work all the harder because of the absence of compulsion, had the opposite effect on the lazy and easy-going;

and I have known some who ran to seed. Their
mornings were wasted, and their visits became social
rather than pastoral; their sermons, like the lectures
of certain Oxford Fellows whom I have known,
were the unrevised performances of earlier years;
and their knowledge, without which sermons tend
to be merely spineless and platitudinous, became
more and more rusty. Compared with the men of
whom I have been speaking, they were what Faber's
'Hark, hark, my soul' is to Wesley's 'Thou hidden
Love of God', sounding nothingness to profundity
and fullness. As is so often the case, this degeneracy
went with a superficial good temper, which sometimes disguised from the victim himself, and from
his friends also, the sad reality: but I think Adam
Clarke would, in these cases, have preferred that the
good temper should have been less natural and
more the product of grace.

It is remarkable how soon a congregation, however little chance it may have had of acquiring
knowledge, will detect the absence of it in the
sermons it hears. It may resent pedantry, but it
likes substance; and it recognizes the solid learning
which may lie behind simplicity. As, according to
Johnson, a very ordinary man, sheltering with
Burke under an archway, would say, 'That is a
great man', so a congregation of ordinary people
knows instinctively when a preacher has based his
sermon on sound study: and, conversely, it cannot
be long deceived by the charlatan. Such men as

I have described were therefore soon found out. Fortunately they were not many in proportion to their more conscientious colleagues.

Actual humbugs and hypocrites were rarer still; and the yearly test—'They were examined one by one'—was always there for them to pass. The examiners, however, pardonably enough, were inclined to temper justice with mercy; and they hesitated to deprive a man of his means of living, and even, in certain cases, to doom him to probable starvation. Here and there, accordingly, and specially in the poorer circuits, were to be found men whose lives were in sad contradiction to their professions: and the contradiction was sometimes only too open and flagrant. A circuit steward once, on a Saturday night, assisted his pastor out of a gutter, and next morning, with amazing charity, listened to a pious discourse without betraying, by word or look, his inner feelings. But it was not always a man capable of keeping a secret who made such discoveries; and the scandal became known not only to Church-members but to the outside public. A Chairman of a District, largely composed of villages, told me once that it was his yearly endeavour, not always successful, to keep 'shady men' out of the circuits under his charge. Since then, I believe, the determination has been strengthened to end the evil at all costs.

I spoke at the beginning of this chapter of the masterfulness of the ministry in former days. I return to the same subject at the close. Masterfulness must not be confused with independence: if it has any connexion with independence at all, it is independence carried too far. One of the dangers of denominations in which the ministry rests entirely on the free laic contributions, is lest there should be too great subservience to the laity, and especially to the richer members. There is, therefore, something to be said for the intrepidity of the ministers of the 'forties', who, though the livelihood of themselves and their families was at the mercy of their congregations, spoke out their thoughts though they must have known they would be unpalatable. In this they were following, though too stringently, the example of John Wesley, who, with total indifference to questions of loss or gain, struck off the membership lists any names, however prominent, of those whose attendance at class, or other conduct, was unsatisfactory: and there is every reason to believe that St. Paul was equally uncompromising.

Here again, though there has been inevitably some infusion of human weakness, I think Methodism may stand comparison with other denominations. The system is a fair compromise between that of Established Churches, in which the position of the clergyman, unless he passes all bounds, is all but impregnable, and that of Churches in which the minister is at the mercy of his congregation. A Methodist minister cannot, like Mr. Edwards in the famous Scottish case which led to the Disruption, be forced on a parish which does not want him; he comes, as a rule, by invitation. Nor, once there, is he there for life: his tenure is revised every year, and a torture known to be terminable can generally be endured.

On the other hand, the minister, belonging to a 'Connexion' or unified society, has his remedy also. If he finds that he is not welcome in one city, he can go to another; and he can rely on the vast force of a nation-wide organization to protect him. Readers of a once-famous novel, Margaret Oliphant's *Salem Chapel*, will remember the troubles of the scholarly Congregational pastor when brought up against the obstinacy and ignorance of a wealthy deacon, on whom the worldly prosperity of Salem mainly depended. Mr. Vincent, too honest to sacrifice his convictions, is finally defeated, and compelled to resign, his place being taken by an accommodating man who gives his public what the public wants, marries the tradesman's daughter, and, along with his Church, flourishes—in externals —like the green bay-tree.

Margaret Oliphant was a member of the Established Kirk of Scotland, and meant in this story to show the advantages of a safe position, buttressed by the State, to a minister of a parish. But she did not prove her point. Had she studied Methodism she might have discovered a Church in which the advantages of the security she found in State support were, to a great extent, gained without the sacrifice

of freedom. Since her time, the Salems, by joining
in a loose federation, have in large measure achieved
the same end, while at the same time maintaining
their great principle of congregational autonomy:
and I think they have done so in imitation of the
Methodist system, with the adaptations demanded
by their own needs.

these walking-sticks.' The parents listened to this sermon with the gravest attention, not showing, by the slightest sign, that they saw anything ludicrous in it; and the child, brought up in this natural manner, took religion as he took his food— tasting that it was good. Children thus trained in the way rarely depart from it.

The family, father, mother, down to babies in arms, regularly went to chapel. Only once, in all my experience, did a preacher resent the crying of a baby—as a rule he hardly seemed to notice it. He preferred the company of a mother, even with occasional disturbance, to her room; and he believed that it was a good thing for the child to grow up with a habit of Church attendance founded in days before memory began. The modern custom of removing children before the sermon, and the gradual disappearance of the family pew, would not have been approved by that generation. Nor were there special children's services; and Wesley's Hymn Book had no section devoted to juveniles. Such things were appropriated to Sunday Schools, the business of which was, so far as I can tell, to prepare the children to understand the following Sunday service, or to paraphrase the preceding into language intelligible to them. In a day school which I attended from the age of six to seven, the mistress always began the Monday morning's lessons with a catechism on the sermon of the day before; and it was extraordinary how much of it had been assimilated. I have a fancy that some modern psychologists, who hold that sermons and theological hymns are not for children, would modify their views if they could bring those days back and listen to those examinations. Even the youngest children remembered *something*. Both the working and the theory of the Sunday School were different, so far as I can see, from what they are to-day. The ideas of secular education, so all-pervasive at present, had not penetrated into these class-rooms.

But, despite all this, many, I think, who have to deal with the young in this twentieth century will feel a twinge of envy as they think of the teachers and parents of old. What motive have they to appeal to when urging their pupils or children in the right direction? As family prayer has ceased, as the knowledge of the Bible has all but vanished, and as religion has, where it has not utterly disappeared, faded into a vague abstraction or been vulgarized into mere formal convention, youth has no anchorage, no lodestar. I have spoken to schoolmasters of long experience, and all say that whereas, when they began, they could speak to their pupils, on religious grounds, with some hope of a response, now they have nothing to say but 'It is not done', no standard but the ordinary rules of the world, no sanction but public opinion, and scarcely any ideal but *esprit de corps* or 'sportsmanship'. Whereas they could, in the past, rely on conscience, they must now describe wrong-doing as 'not cricket'; and the results are not satisfying. Arnold may have had his limitations and his faults; but is there a Head Master to-day who could address his school, as Arnold did, with the words, 'It does not matter if this school has three hundred boys, or a hundred, or fifty, but it does matter that it should be a school of Christian gentlemen'? How many parents, vastly easier as they are than their own parents in their relations with their children, can guide them to 'the city of habitation' with any sense of possessing a reliable map of the route? And, if they pause and think, are they contented with themselves, or do they feel quite happy about their children's future? Having renounced religion as such a guide, are they sure they have found a sufficing substitute? It may be that, when religion is gone, its worth will be perceived, as, in Jean Paul Richter's *Dream*, when in place of the divine eye there was but an empty socket, the universe was lonely. 'It so falls out', says the Friar in Shakespeare,

> 'That what we have we prize not to the worth
> Whiles we enjoy it, but, being lacked and lost,
> Why, then we rack the value, then we find
> The virtue that possession would not show us
> Whiles it was ours.'

CHAPTER IV

THE BUSINESS MAN

As I HAVE ALREADY HINTED, there were two things
which 'made' the business-man, the factory-owner,
and in general the commerce of Britain in the early
nineteenth century. The first was what Arnold
Toynbee called, in imitation of the great French
upheaval, the 'Industrial Revolution', and the
second was the principle which that Revolution
inspired and from which in its turn it received
inspiration, 'laissez-faire', a hint to governments
not to meddle. Let business look after itself, and it
will make its way. Incidentally, tax its profits as
little as possible, and—in the long run—both
business and the public revenue will profit. This
principle Pitt had dimly seen ; Peel, the son of a great
manufacturer, had seen it more clearly; and
Gladstone carried it to full lengths.

To support and defend this system, a science of
economics, developed by Ricardo and others, was
constructed, along with a science of politics elabor-
ated by Jeremy Bentham. Ricardo, to simplify his
problem, treated men as merely money-making
animals : with what they might be besides he did
not, as an economist, concern himself. He was like

a geometer who, in investigating the properties of lines, neglects their breadth and thickness, with the result that his conclusions are much less complicated than they might be. Or, to use a comparison more relevant to the case, he was a theorist in ballistics who should disregard friction and the resistance of the air. Unluckily friction is even more common in human relations than in the motions of solids; and, so far from being an accident in the social problem, is of its very essence. The most avaricious of men does not always act from love of money, and there are many in whom love of money does not exist at all. Nevertheless, a system in which men are treated as avaricious by Nature tends to be regarded as a defence of avarice, just as Machiavelli's treatise on the best way to become a tyrant tends to be regarded as a panegyric on tyranny.

In the view of Bentham, government was a necessary evil, and the less of its working we saw the better. Nearly all its interferences with ordinary life were mischievous. It meddled with religion, and the result was persecution on one side and hypocrisy on the other. It meddled with trade, and invariably with disastrous effect. It was noteworthy that the few Acts of Parliament which were undoubtedly good had been usually those repealing previous Acts; and it would plainly therefore have been advantageous to the country to dispense with the bad and thus avoid the necessity of passing the good. Especially bad were Acts restraining the 'liberty' of the individual, who as a rule knew far more about his own interests than the grandmotherly State which tried to manage his affairs for him. Books were written showing the very narrow limits within which the State's control ought to be exercised; and it was proved, again and again, that the State had no business to control the manner in which men might become rich. That other men might become poor in the process was not emphasized. A very popular expression of these ideas may be seen in Macaulay's Essay on Southey's Colloquies; and this is the more remarkable as Macaulay, while thus expounding Bentham's views, thought himself an anti-Benthamite. The spirit of the age was too strong for him; he might oppose the theorist but he accepted the theory.

Now, when philosophers contrive to gain a popular hearing for their philosophy, and when it spreads from the class-room to the street, it is practically always misunderstood, and is applied without those necessary qualifications which its originators have been careful to mark. We see this truth exemplified to-day in the case of the semi-science of Psychology and the theory of Relativity. Journalists borrow the stock-phrases of Freud and Einstein, and employ them with appalling inaccuracy; and people everywhere talk of complexes and of electrons without any real comprehension of either. Novelists aid the delusion—that there has been a great advance in knowledge—by the skilful use of a technical dialect, and both they and their readers imagine themselves profound thinkers because their words are unintelligible.

This is bad enough when the philosophy is of merely theoretical interest; but the effects are far worse when it can also be turned to practical uses. If, for example, the Copernican system of astronomy is applied by mere amateurs to the art of navigation, wrecks will be frequent. And, when the Benthamite doctrine of 'laissez-faire', or the Ricardian system of economics, was adopted, greedily and hastily, by factory-owners in the interest of the exploitation of the masses, it is obvious that errors would enter which would be extremely disastrous. Such a philosophy could easily be twisted into a justification of the most selfish avarice, and would enable a man to pride himself on his nobility when he was really base, or to regard himself as a missionary of progress, when in actual fact he was a pioneer of barbarism. Private vices might easily appear to him as public benefits, and ere long would cease to be considered vices at all. This, in many cases, is what did happen, and indeed has not yet ceased to happen. Tyrants, in all sincerity, deemed themselves philanthropists, and, while grinding the faces of the poor, imagined they were doing service at once to God and to men.

We must not cast the sole blame on the publicists and economists who were thus adopted as teachers. Ricardoism and Benthamism were but suffering a common fate. Neither Ricardo nor Bentham was in any sense personally inhumane. Both were aiming at 'the greatest happiness of the greatest number'; and yet their theories, carried out into action by men who misapprehended them, often produced a vast preponderance of misery. Employers hastened to adopt them: here was a Decalogue which bade them do exactly what they were doing and desired to continue to do.

These men were not more wicked than others; they were not born with a double dose of original sin. Some of them were sincerely religious; and the great majority would have been genuinely astonished if their uprightness and honesty had been doubted. We shall all, if we examine ourselves closely, see that we are inclined to identify our own advantage with righteousness—only we rarely do thus examine ourselves: and the early factory-owners and masters were like us. Every man's character is conditioned by his circumstances, and, where his own interests are concerned, he will 'first endure, then pity, then embrace', a course which, to those not exposed to his temptations, seems almost ostentatiously atrocious.

Hence the ruthless treatment of the factory-worker, which stirs our astonishment as we read of it in the official reports. Hence the opposition to the Factory Acts, led by men like Bright and Cobden, and moving the indignation of Shaftesbury and his friends. Child-mortality, deaths caused by unfenced machinery, semi-starvation through low wages and the truck-system, all these things were defended as part and parcel of the Providential order. In vain did Michael Sadler point out that there was no liberty of contract when a man must take what was offered him or perish, that 'laissez-faire' for the master meant savage compulsion for the 'hand' —a designation only too significant. The wealth of the country at large depended on the sacrifice of these unfortunates; a victory cannot be won without casualties in the rank and file; and there were the words of Christ that the poor we have always with us. As the Southerners saw in slavery a manifestation of the will of God, so these purchasers of 'freemen' averred, with sincerity, that they were but instruments of the divine Purpose.

I met in my youth mill-owners who would point out, with more than the pride of Adam Smith discoursing on pin-making, the advantages of division of labour, and who would show how the whole time of a single girl would be taken up with the mechanical performance of a single action. It never occurred to them to think of the mental and moral results of such monotony. Similarly, I have known well-to-do shop-keepers who never thought of providing seats for their sales-people. It was enough if they paid the wages. And yet on Sundays they would read that the righteous man is merciful to his beast. To many of them the ill-health of a worker was a crime, and the criminal would at once

be thrown on the scrap-heap. Such was the system,
and those whom it did not suit must take their fate.
Was not the trade of the country advancing by leaps
and bounds? Were not profits increasing? and did
not a considerable proportion of them go in
charities and other good causes? Did not they
support the Poor Law? So strongly were these views
held, and so widely did they penetrate, that I was
confidently assured by an eminent minister of the
gospel, whose congregation consisted largely of
these men and their families, that it was impossible
for anyone to starve in England. He had unconsciously imbibed the ideas of his business
friends, and was as fully convinced as they that all
was well in this best of all possible worlds.

Strikes, and Trades Unions, were in themselves
wrong, quite apart from any of the incidental evils
which might accompany them. The final legislation
which gave the Unions their position was passed,
not by the party which these men generally supported, but by Disraeli's Government, which rested
largely on the agricultural interest; and it was
openly said that the Factory Laws were passed by
that interest in revenge for the repeal of the Corn
Laws. It is true that there was a beam in the
agricultural eye; for the treatment of the country-
labourer was certainly no better than that of the
factory-hand. But, as usual, each side saw only the
mote in the eye of its neighbour: and both sides
thought themselves religious. One went to chapel,

the other to church, and both prayed with equal devotion.

But this is by no means the whole story. Towards the end of the 'fifties' a cloud might have been seen in the distance, at first no larger than a human hand. Material prosperity was gradually seen to be not everything, and the Industrial Revolution was timidly suspected as hardly the dawn of the millennium. Ere long man began to assail 'Manchesterism', at first recklessly and crudely, as Tennyson assailed it in *Maud*, even glorifying war as an improvement on the chase of gain. 'Who but a fool would have faith in a tradesman's ware or his word? When Timour-Mammon grins on a pile of children's bones, better loud war by land and by sea, war with a thousand battles, and shaking a hundred thrones.' This of course was wild denunciation, and Tennyson, called to account for it, had to defend it as 'mono-dramatic'. But the evils, though certainly war did not put an end to them—the contractors for the Crimean adventure saw to that—were being recognized, and remedies were being sought. The 'Song of the Shirt' and the 'Cry of the Children' appeared in the same year, and produced their effect. Philanthropists of every kind, some sentimental, some practical, made their voices heard; and among the practical philanthropists were some of the masters themselves, to whom reform meant a monetary loss. At the same time, there was a change in economic theory.

There is a marked difference in tone and substance between the cold mathematics of Ricardo and the humane, sympathetic economics of John Stuart Mill, in whose book there is a clear recognition that the actors in the social sphere are not pawns but men of flesh and blood. The iron rigidity of the old laws was relaxed, and Political Economy to a great extent ceased to deserve Carlyle's mocking nickname, the 'Dismal Science'. Mill, indeed, went much further than Carlyle in true humanity. 'While Carlyle', said he, 'preaches the gospel of work, I with equal fervour preach the gospel of leisure.' Letting alone was still the rule, but it admitted of 'numerous abatements and exceptions', all of which had to do with the checking of tyranny, oppression, trickery, and all the devices by which the wealthy can injure or circumvent the poor. We actually find, in treatises on money, many applications to social philosophy, and paragraphs devoted to education. I spoke a little time since of Macaulay's youthful advocacy of 'laissez-faire'. Within fifteen years he, the most 'Victorian' of men, whose famous Third Chapter is a glorification of material progress, was strongly supporting the Ten Hours Bill, crying out for the education of the masses, and proclaiming that Government must be something more than a mere hangman; it had duties to perform for its people, to safeguard their health, to improve their morals, to widen their outlook; and, as an aid to all this, to better their physical surroundings.

Novelists, giving their public what it wanted, were making known the actual state of things, and at times demanding reform. Even *The Family Herald* raised its voice in the cause, though it 'shunned politics'. Of the work of Dickens, and of his clearly expressed opinions, which were not always self-consistent but were always benevolent, there is no need to speak. By common consent he was among the very chiefest agents in raising the level of social life that his age and country knew. Daniel Webster, the great American orator and statesman, said in public that Dickens had effected more in this field than all the newspapers and politicians put together; and the famous Nonconformist divine, Baldwin Brown, ranked the novels, as engines of social reform, with the London City Mission and the cholera. Dickens, said Ruskin, 'though he chose to speak in a circle of stage fire, was entirely right in his main drift and purpose in every book he had written'; and Ruskin chose, as perhaps the best, in this respect, of all the novels, *Hard Times*—the very story which appeared to Macaulay a mass of 'sullen socialism'. Dickens did not understand economics, and he treated the science unfairly; but no man did more to compel the economists to reconsider their principles.

The mention of Ruskin reminds me of the enormous, and on the whole salutary, sensation aroused by this great writer's economic writings, and especially by the four short essays contributed in

1860 to the *Cornhill Magazine*, and republished in 1862 under the title *Unto this Last*. They met with violent antagonism, and were certainly, as was not rare with Ruskin's books, provocative enough. A fairly innocent dictum of Adam Smith's drew from him the comment, 'I request any Christian reader to think within himself what an entirely damned state of mind any human creature must have got into, who could read with acceptance such a statement as this'; and there were other diatribes equally violent. But the book, on the whole, was emphatically noble and magnanimous, if not—to use Ruskin's own favourite adverb—'entirely' so. It recalls everywhere the spirit, and constantly the very language, of the ancient Hebrew prophets, and is in fact a long homily on the words of Amos, 'I will not turn away their punishment, because they have sold the righteous for silver, and the needy for a pair of shoes'. Its force lay mainly in its insistence on the contradiction between the Christian professions of the nation and its heathen behaviour. 'Nothing in history has ever been so disgraceful to human intellect as the acceptance among us of the common doctrines of political economy as a science. I know no previous instance of a nation's establishing a systematic disobedience to the first principles of its professed religion. The writings which we (verbally) esteem as divine, not only denounce the love of money as the source of all evil, and as an idolatry abhorred of the Deity, but declare

Mammon-worship to be the accurate and irreconcilable opposite of God's service : and, whenever they speak of riches absolute, and poverty absolute, declare woe to the rich, and blessing to the poor. Whereupon we forthwith investigate a science of becoming rich, as the shortest road to national prosperity.'

When prophets, novelists, and thinkers, who, as ever, at once reflected and moulded public opinion, spoke in this manner, it was inevitable that the men specially concerned should ask themselves somewhat pointed questions. Hundreds of thousands read *Hard Times*, and among them captains of industry, many of whom were conscientious men, who began to wonder whether there was not something of Mr. Bounderby, hitherto unsuspected, in themselves. Ruskin's books—in accordance with his principle that good things should command a good price—were expensive, but seventy or eighty thousand copies of *Unto this Last* were sold, and reached the minds of many business-men, multitudes of whom were sincerely Christian, though they had, perhaps, not hitherto sufficiently considered their position. They naturally resented Ruskin's exaggerated attacks, and regarded him as no less of a caricaturist than Dickens himself. They knew that they were not cheats and hypocrites; Scrooge and Marley were no more typical of their class than the murderer Jasper was a typical Church-musician. When they picked up a pamphlet called *Business is*

Business, and read that the sellers of milk sold chalk and water, and the sellers of boots were dealers in manipulated paper, they laughed or scowled according to their dispositions. But they did begin to consider whether there might not be a grain of truth in the denunciations, and whether their business-principles and course of conduct were really consistent with the Christianity they professed, and in which they really believed. 'Him whom they ignorantly worshipped, Ruskin was declaring unto them'; and the revelation produced its effect. Not, of course, that there were not many who went scornfully on in their old ways. I am speaking not of those who deliberately made evil good, but of the well-meaning, whose eyes were now enlightened, and who, discovering to their surprise that they had been worshipping Mammon too faithfully, resolved to change their deity. Some, as I have said, compromised, like the old English kings in the early days of our Christianity, who set up an altar to Thor at one end of the church, and the Sacramental Table at the other. They kept up the old habits on week-days, and went to the sanctuary on Sunday. But many—and I knew several personally—were as 'entirely honest merchants' as Ruskin always maintained his own father to have been. Solomon himself would have been satisfied with them; their balances were just, the wages they paid were good, and they stood *in loco parentis* to their workpeople. So far as they valued success in business, it was not from avarice, but from the sense that it was a sign of work well done and duly rewarded: riches and honour are in the left hand of Wisdom.

Philosophy follows conduct, as conduct follows philosophy. It was not long, therefore, before we began to see a remarkable and progressive change of tone in the scientific economists. It had, as I remarked, begun in 1848 with John Stuart Mill; and even Ruskin admitted that Mill had shown humanity, though asserting that every touch of humanity was inconsistent with his diabolic theory. But now there arose theorists who, in their basic principles, provided for a society, not of money-grubbing robots, but of human beings with mixed motives. It was said by some that Adam Smith himself had been of this mind. In his *Wealth of Nations* he had, for the sake of simplification, assumed that men were moved by avarice only; but this was *merely* a simplification. In his *Moral Sentiments* he had given the other side, and added new factors to his equations. Whether this was true or not, the new economic school, at first tentatively, then more freely, combined Adam Smith's two works into a single volume: until at last we had Marshall's *Economics of Industry* and Arnold Toynbee's *Lectures*, in which there was full recognition that a man cannot be split up into independent fragments, one selfish, another altruistic, acting, like the 'humorous' characters of Ben Jonson, isolated rôles on the stage of the mind. The economics of the

future were to be Shakespearian, not Jonsonian;
the men of whom the science spoke were not to be
so possessed by a single passion that 'it doth draw

> All his effects, his spirits, and his powers,
> In their confluctions, all to run one way';

they were to be as complicate and wonderful as a
Shylock or a Hamlet.

Gradually the effect of all this became visible. I
knew a man who had read *Unto this Last* in 1862
with unmitigated repugnance. He read it again
twenty years later, and said to me, 'It is strange,
but Ruskin now seems to me absolutely right: and
the world is better so far as it has obeyed his
preachings'. This man was a factory-owner. What
he had been like in that capacity in the 'sixties' I do
not know; but in the 'eighties' he was a model
master, poorer in the things of this world than he
had been, but as 'passing rich' in other ways as
Goldsmith's clergyman. He was by no means
unique. Had there been many like him, I think the
friction between workers and employers, of which
there has been so much in the last fifty years, might
have been less virulent. What is perhaps even more
important, there would have been less hatred of
Christianity in the working-classes. For that hatred,
and it was intense, was largely due to the belief that
Political Economy and Christianity were two sides of
the same thing, or at least two allies supporting each
other. As in the old days it was No Bishop, No

King, so now it was commonly said, No Church, No wage-tyranny. A clergyman was looked on as the dog-collared abettor of the manufacturing exploiter. Nothing exasperated men like Bradlaugh more than to hear a parson bid them submit to their miseries as to the will of God—the will of God turning out, on investigation, to be the law of supply and demand. If this was Christianity, they would have none of it; and hence the rapid growth of 'Secularism' in the country—a popular form of doctrine which insisted that religion should stop talking about the blessings of the next world and pay some attention to the evils of this one. When therefore Ruskin and his followers came and asserted that Ricardoism, so far from being Christianity, was the negation of Christianity, they were helping to reconcile the labouring classes with religion. They were not, I think, quite fair in their denuncia-tions, but they were none the less effective on that account; and when some masters began to act according to these principles, the effect was still more marked.

In the 'eighties', indeed, the translation of these principles into action might have been seen on a very hopeful scale. It was then that, largely under the influence of Arnold Toynbee and others, who were economic theorists, but could see little use in theories which were confined to the study, a movement began the object of which was to improve by every possible means the physical condition of

the masses, while at the same time emphasizing in
every way the brotherhood of all men. There was
to be no condescension in the more fortunate, and
an endeavour was to be made to end the suspicion
and shyness with which the less fortunate regarded
their helpers. Some of the most promising University scholars joined this movement; and, though
it was to some extent checked by the wave of
Imperialism which succeeded, it has never died out.
It is not, of course, precisely a business-movement;
but in so far as it promotes good feeling between
masters and men, it contributes its share to national
prosperity.

When one considers the state of things which
prevails at present, the endless disputes between
masters and men, the strikes, the constant abuse of
capital on one side and of labour on the other, one
might easily imagine that if the movement I have
alluded to brought about improvement, what went
before must have been bad indeed. I do not wish
to minimize the miseries of the 'thirties', nor do I
wish to exaggerate the advance made between the
'sixties' and the 'eighties'. Inveterate evils cannot
be cured in a few years: and the memory of old
grievances constantly survives to maintain hatred
and suspicion long after the grievances have been
removed. A man who has heard from his grand-
father of the Hungry Forties, of the hateful penalties
imposed on the Chartists or the Tolpuddle
Labourers, and of the tyrannies of factory-owners

in the 'fifties', is only too likely to be rancorous and intransigent in the conflicts of our time. But things are unquestionably somewhat better. Men meet and discuss, on more equal terms than of old. Complaints are listened to; and public opinion often exerts a compelling influence on the most obstinate Die-hards. No magnate dare now say, 'Cannot I do what I will with my own?' and on the other hand a strike which cannot convince the public that its cause is just is bound to fail. A certain element of justice has entered into these quarrels: they are no longer decided on Ricardian principles. We hear less and less of supply and demand, and more and more of equity. There is still much to be done; masters and men may still say with the remorseful Henry V:

> More will I do,
> Though all that I can do is nothing worth,
> Since that my penitence comes after all,
> Imploring pardon.

And penitence is the first step in religion.

CHAPTER V

HOW THEY READ THE BIBLE

THE SOCIETY I have been describing, whatever its cultural limitations, had one great advantage which the present generation, to its serious loss, has largely denied itself. It knew its Bible. Apart from the Church or Chapel services, with their First and Second Lessons, family prayer, with its Old Testament chapter in the morning, and its New Testament in the evening, made the Victorian Evangelical acquainted with the chief passages in some of the greatest literature in the world, and with some of the greatest episodes in history: and the children were encouraged to read the Book in private also. When, years later, I came across Ruskin's account of the way in which his parents drilled him in scriptural knowledge, I recognized the vestiges of my own youth; and I should imagine many scores of Nonconformists could have drawn the same parallel. The results of this constant study were remarkable. I remember an occasion on which, as the family was about to go for its summer holiday, every copy of the Bible had been packed up—for such copies were more necessary than buckets, spades, or sandshoes. But the lesson was given nevertheless. A boy of seventeen stood up, and recited the eighth chapter of Romans from beginning to end—with, it is true, a little prompting from the father. The Bible was a stock quotation-book, and the slightest references to it were appreciated. At a school which I attended, a boy of an argumentative turn had overslept himself, and was late to early-morning school. He made his defence in a long-winded manner, and indeed endeavoured to keep up a debate with the master for a considerable time. The master closed the discussion with the words, 'The sluggard is wiser in his own conceit than seven men who can render a reason';[1] and there was an instant burst of laughter, for nearly every boy in the form knew the source of the quotation. Much later in life, I happened to be present when an old minister called on a retired business-man at meal-time. Seeing the family at table, he wished to leave, but the gentleman pressed him to stay. 'No', said he with a smile, 'withdraw thy foot from thy neighbour's house.' The man recognized the passage at once, and, saying, 'I shall never weary of *thee* and so hate thee', added, 'Friend, come up higher', and made him sit at his right side. Seeing that it was likely to pour with rain all day, a child of seven said

---

[1] The reader will recall the indignant exclamation of the infant Macaulay when the maid had taken away his stones from his little garden, 'Cursed be Sally, for it is written, Cursed is he that removeth his neighbour's landmark!' I could parallel this. A child, receiving his first toothbrush, remarked, 'The Lord hath given us cleanness of teeth in all our cities'—a recent lesson in family prayer having been the fourth chapter of Amos.

to his mother, 'Mother, it is like the contentious woman'.

A boy was once quarrelling with his elder brother, and indulging in expressions of contempt; whereupon the insulted youth took him by the arm, and turned him out of the room, remarking, 'Cast out the scorner and contention shall go out'. Another, aged nine, once told his mother, à propos of nothing, that he hated her; the explanation being that he had taken the words of Christ about 'hating one's father and mother' too literally.

Sometimes, indeed, I think older people applied these quotations a little unfairly. Some children having been disturbing their father by playing noisily, he remarked with a tragic air, 'If you go on like this, you will bring down my grey hairs with sorrow to the grave'; and the children wept at the terrible thought. A lad I knew called his sister a fool. But she was equal to it. 'Whosoever calleth his brother a fool is in danger of hell-fire.' Though the boy retorted that nothing was said about sisters, he yet felt that this was a poor subterfuge, and resolved to limit himself in future to the milder word 'Raca'. I have heard conversations kept up for a considerable time with hardly a sentence which was not scriptural; and capping Bible verses was a common Sunday game. I knew people who could repeat the genealogy from Adam to Christ as accurately as Scott's friend, John Leyden; and others who could, in middle life, name the

kings of Israel and Judah with the years of their
reigns. 'Quod semel est imbuta recens, servabit
odorem testa diu.'[1]

As I hinted above, and as indeed goes without
saying, such knowledge is of high literary value.
It is impossible to appreciate some of the greatest
English writers unless the Bible is at one's finger-
ends. Not to mention Milton, Fuller, or the
Puritan writers generally, the overt or disguised
Biblical quotations in Chaucer, Lamb, Macaulay,
Ruskin, and scores of others, are a main element in
their force: and the present times of ignorance,
which are so lamentably winked at, inevitably miss
that force. Only the other day I came across a
gruesome error as to Dryden's Achitophel in no less
a book than M. Maurois' *History of England*. As if
David had not sons enough already, M. Maurois
made Achitophel a brother of Absalom, and, what
is far more inexcusable, his translator passed the
mistake, though it occurred twice, without notice.
But what becomes of Dryden's satire if the Biblical
allusions and parallels are thus ignored? The
Victorians whom I knew had access to a region of
pleasure to which even M. Maurois is a stranger:
and, if they knew, as many did know, little other

---

[1] Some time ago, being unable to sleep, I happened to think that the
names of the Patriarchs in Genesis v. would be a good substitute for sheep
going through a hedge. I do not suppose I had thought of these for forty
years; but I recovered them all, with their numbers. This suggested a
theory of these numbers which I sent to the *Expository Times*, and which
attracted some attention. I imagine that there were many ministers'
children who could have performed a similar feat; for we were encouraged
to regard these digits as sacred, and to ponder over them again and again.

literature, what they did know was the best. Their shelves were like those which, according to Cowley, could be seen in the Prophets' College at Ramah:

In the library a few choice authors stood,
Yet 'twas well-stored, for that small store was good.

In some of the poorer houses the 'store' might be merely a Bible and a hymn book; but it would be hard to find two books of equal literary power. If the cottager was a Methodist, the hymn book would be Wesley's; and any impartial scholar who will glance through that book will soon see, perhaps with surprise, that it is not only a collection of verses to be sung, but a carefully arranged theological treatise, 'a little body', as Wesley called it, 'of experimental and practical divinity'. But it is even more. It is a learned book, crowded, hardly less notably than the Odes of Gray himself, with apt quotations from all sources, from Ignatius, from Augustine, from Milton, from Dryden, from Prior; and the congregations which used it gained insensibly a very considerable amount of knowledge, and imbibed at the same time a certain critical taste. That this is true can be shown in a thousand ways. Let one example be sufficient. There is a Cornish story, drawn direct from the life, called *Daniel Quorm and his Religious Notions*. Daniel Quorm is a simple cottager, whose 'notions' are derived exclusively from the Bible and the Hymn Book. You may not agree with them all, but you cannot deny

that they are ordered, consistent, and often profound. He is a theologian, practical yet mystical;
and he has always ready, for the help of others or for
the confutation of 'error', a passage either from
Scripture or—what is often the same thing—from a
favourite hymn. What ordinary cottager would
quote, as the expression of his highest feelings, such
a couplet as

> Plunged in the Godhead's deepest sea,
> And lost in Thine immensity?

Anyone familiar with the Methodism of fifty or sixty
years since would own that the Daniel Quorms,
though rare, existed in many places, and that the
picture is no exaggeration.

And yet it must be confessed that, while the Bible
was thus known, it was known all wrong. There was
practically no scientific study of it; no conception
that, as Jowett put the point somewhat provo-
catively in *Essays and Reviews*, the Bible should be
read like any other book. Still less, if possible, was
it understood that it should be read as a *literature*,
and that the relation of each part of that literature
to the rest should be grasped. The method used
was often hardly better than the old one of picking
our 'Sortes' by chance, such as Dinah Morris
employed when in doubt as to marrying Adam
Bede. The Book was read in scraps, sometimes no
longer than single verses torn from their context,
and these were interpreted as ancient soothsayers

interpreted the scattered Sibylline leaves. The verse, thus selected by lot, was an oracle, and was tortured into meaning what its author could never have meant, and applied to the circumstances of the guesser's own life in the most reckless fashion. What was almost as bad, there were many who, urged on by vanity and their parents' encouragement, read the Bible through—unluckily from beginning to end, without regard to chronological order, and without reference to a good commentary. I knew one family that actually calculated the number of *verses* to be read each day in order to finish the task in a year. Discovering that sixty-four verses would thus complete the Old Testament, and twenty-one the New, they actually kept up this mechanical system for several months. As for any idea that, for example, Genesis is a composite work, there was not the slightest; nor was much favour shown to those who, feebly and tentatively, tried to think of the characters as human beings. Milman's description of Abraham as 'a great sheikh' was still spoken of with horror; and Stanley's *Jewish Church*, mild and timid as was its liberalism, made its way but gradually into ministerial houses.

Still worse, perhaps, in its effects was the prevailing belief in literal inspiration, and the almost Rabbinic fancy that the sacred text had been, as it were, *constructed* into a kind of cryptogram, so that, if the words could be *made* to mean something, that something *was* the meaning. That particular word, it was held, could not have been used instead of a synonym without a special intention; and we were at liberty to strain it to the uttermost. The preachers were here not without blame. The old Puritan who, wishing to denounce women's head-gear, picked out 'Top-knot come down' from 'Let him that is in the house-top not come down', was hardly more daring than some of the preachers I have 'sat under'. Macaulay refers to a sermon he heard on the single word 'Therefore': I could easily match this from my own experiences. There was, even in the 'nineties', a powerful discourse on the word 'How', and another, in which 'This is that' was taken from Stephen's 'This is that Moses' and distorted into a paradox of profound significance. No conjunction of vocables was allowed to pass as trivial or accidental; all had been determined from time immemorial in the divine counsels. Nor was it only the 'unlearned and unstable' who thus wrested these Scriptures to their own destruction. As late as 1902 I listened, with mingled amusement and annoyance, to a clergyman, who afterwards became an Archbishop, as he chased through the Old Testament the various occurrences of the simple adverb 'Notwithstanding', and drew from them some very astonishing lessons. I was reminded of the very similar treatment to which Shakespeare has been subjected by devotees who study him not wisely but too well: though Shakespeare, idolized as he has been, is not proclaimed as the vehicle of plenary inspiration. I should never cease if I retailed the whole list of eccentricities of this kind which throng my memory: they are multitudinous, and of every possible kind. A minister I knew drew up, though he never preached, a sketch of a sermon, with introduction, three parts, and a conclusion, on ' As well the singers as the players on instruments shall be there; All my springs are in thee'—that is, 'Full choir and orchestra, to the tune Springs'. Another did actually discourse on 'The Prayers of David the son of Jesse are ended', as if this simple 'Finis' harboured some occult doctrine; nor were these the only colophons which have earned the undeserved honour of a forty minutes' homiletic commentary. I remember more than one sermon on 'Jesus only', in which the preachers, totally disregarding the fact that the three Apostles saw only Jesus because there was no one else to see, expatiated with vigorous eloquence on the duty of their hearers to see 'Jesus only' in the crowded streets of London. It is true these devices were sometimes ingenious, and they may have been adopted, on occasion, to catch a startled attention. The famous Dr. Parker once preached on Peter's words, 'I go a-fishing'. He first gave out the text, and then, in his compelling voice, twice repeated the 'I'. Apparently what Peter implied was, 'You others may doubt and dawdle, but *I* mean business, and instant business'. 'We want', said the Doctor, 'a few more of these I's—and then others will follow them.' It was a clever discourse; but there was at least one in the audience who knew that the word 'I' is so unemphatic in the original that it is not even expressed, and who feared some others might fancy that this sublime egoism was really ascribed to Peter by the evangelist.

This being the attitude of the more learned, the state of mind of the simple may be imagined. I once asked a pious friend what he made of the text, 'For Parbar westward, four at the causeway and two at Parbar': and the answer was that there must be a mystical meaning in it which would be revealed some day. Though Adam Clarke had written a commentary, it was doubtful whether he had not been wasting his time; for a certain spiritual insight was a far surer guide to the understanding of the Word than a knowledge of Greek and Hebrew. Nor, indeed, was an intellectual comprehension in the least necessary. Thus I have seen good people at family prayer listening intently, with faces reminding one of Beatrice as she gazed at the sun, to the reading of passages from Colossians or Ephesians, of which it is certain they could not have given a rational account of a single word. The sound of the words had an hypnotic influence, and exerted a charm like that of Merlin's woven paces and waving hands.

This Fundamentalism or Daytonianism—though neither name had as yet been invented—was usually taken quietly for granted, but it was some-

H

times deliberately taught, more especially when
'heretical' writings, like *Ecce Homo*, Frank Newman's
Phases of Faith, or those of Carlyle and Ruskin,
began stealthily to make their way into Evangelical
circles. I recall how the saying of Carlyle, 'Things
are not true because they are in the Bible; they are
in the Bible because they are true', was discussed,
somewhat dubiously, by two ministers in my
presence, and its hidden implications were probed
with care. An antidote was felt to be necessary, and,
though so young that I shall not reveal my age, I
was set to read a book called, somewhat pedantic-
ally, *Theopneustia*[1] by a Swiss professor named
Gaussen. Gaussen held and defended the most
rigid theory of plenary inspiration with complete
and unflinching intrepidity. Every word was
inspired, and all were equally inspired. Faced with
the differences between the various Gospel reports
of Christ's actions or speeches, he met the case by
asserting that they were accurate and exact tran-
scripts of what had been repeatedly said or done,
on similar occasions, at sundry times, and in divers
manners. No allowance was made for the idiosyn-
crasies of the Evangelists themselves, who were
simply mouthpieces of the Spirit: and it was therefore right to extract every grain of meaning from
the use of one particular word rather than another.
As to the thousands of various readings—for, though

[1] 'All Scripture is *Theopneustos*, given by inspiration of God,' 2 Timothy iii.
16. I do not know that the word Theopneustia is really Greek.

Gaussen wrote before Lachmann or Westcott and Hort, he was familiar with Griesbach—it was plain that he was perplexed, and his reasoning assumed a sophistical tinge. He was obliged to admit the variations, and, though he claimed with truth that they are nearly always trifling, he was in no better case, for he had throughout insisted that trifles were important. So far as I remember, he concluded that the true and original readings, if only, by some miracle, they could be certainly discovered, were the directly dictated phrases of God. The writers, in fact, were controlled by the Holy Spirit, the copyists unfortunately not. Even when Paul said, 'In this speak I, not the Lord', he was told by the Lord to say that the Lord did not say it. This book, I believe, had a wide and powerful influence, and a most mischievous one. But while the fancy was bad as applied to the New Testament, it was worse as applied to the Old; for it meant the defence of falsehood and cruelty in the name of piety. That fatal confusion which led the Puritans to utilize the Hebrew treatment of the Moabites and Ammonites as a pattern for their own treatment of the 'Malignants', still confused the minds of Victorian Evangelicals. There was a famous and popular book by John Kitto, called *Daily Bible Illustrations*, in which the most dubious acts of Hebrew captains were tortuously excused or approved. It contained, for instance, two chapters, the titles of which sufficiently explain their contents: 'Hebrew Right to Canaan, what it was', and 'Hebrew Right to Canaan, what it was not'; and these 'rights' were held to justify the savage massacres, exterminations, and burnings which marked the conquering path of Joshua and the Judges. There was no conception of the progressive nature of Revelation. The God of the Patriarchs was the God of Jesus, and one truth was clear, whatever He did was right. Even when He was not mentioned, He was still present. 'God not in the Book of Esther!' exclaimed Kitto. He is not named, but He is in every verse, and not least in those verses which tell how the Jews slaughtered thousands of people who had done them no harm. The result was a chaotic farrago of ethical ideas in the minds of those to whom these views came as authoritative: a farrago less harmful, fortunately, than it had been in the days of the Civil Wars, but pregnant with the possibilities of evil.[1]

It must not be thought that these were exclusively Evangelical notions. Readers of Tractarian and High Church works know that they were held equally by men to whom Evangelicalism was anathema. Pusey's *Daniel* endeavoured to show that the prophecy dated from Belshazzar's time, and the

---

[1] To take but one example from the Caroline days. David Leslie, the Scottish General, surprised a body of Macdonalds, and captured three hundred of them. Leslie was a merciful man, and wished to spare them: but the Covenanting minister, to whom 'malignants' were Amalekites, thundered out the words of Samuel, 'What meaneth the bleating of sheep in mine ears, and the lowing of cattle which I hear?' and denounced the General as a disobedient Saul. Leslie had to give way, and the prisoners were hewn, like Agag, in pieces before the Lord.

Professor of Hebrew explained away all the Persian and Greek words, and refused to see the anachronisms which his theory involved. Newman, though renouncing the rest of his early Low Church views, retained his literalism. Rome was, in this respect, in harmony with the Plymouth Brethren. Pius IX declared that the Hebrews, in putting Jericho and Ai to the 'herem', or in hanging the five kings till sunset, were impelled by a passionate faith in the doctrine of the Immaculate Conception. Perrone, the Catholic apologist, in defending the Romanist attitude towards the Bible, applied to Scripture study the words of God to Eve about the Tree of Knowledge, 'Ye shall not eat thereof, lest ye die'; and used the curse of the serpent, which he mistranslated, '*She* shall bruise thy head', as referring to the Virgin Mary. Nay, the Catholic ascription of practical inerrancy to the Vulgate translation, which not only is sometimes incorrect but occasionally bases itself on a false text, makes Catholics even more liable to error than the Fundamentalist who treats the Authorised Version as the immediate voice of God.

Such Fundamentalism, of course, was especially common among the ignorant, who, knowing the Authorised Version—I was almost saying, 'knowing it too well'—regarded any criticism of it as little short of blasphemy. A scholarly minister, in a sermon I heard, ventured to point out that the translators had in a certain passage missed the force

of the original. There was indignation in the
audience. 'As if the Bible was written in Greek!'
was an outraged comment. When the Revised
Version appeared in 1881, the antagonism it excited
was largely due to an uneasy feeling that it was
undermining the foundations of the faith, and if
the foundations were destroyed, what should the
righteous do? It revealed that many things were
uncertain which had been considered irrefragable,
and, by innumerable alterations, distorted the
Divine Word. These good people not only felt, like
the more literate, though without being able
clearly to express their feelings, that the old 'familiar
rhythms' had been wantonly destroyed, but were
convinced that somehow the scholars had treacher-
ously dealt a blow at their dearest beliefs. For this,
again, their teachers were in some measure responsible; during many years past they had, even where
they themselves were fully aware of the real state
of things, shirked the duty of explaining it to their
congregations. Not many were like the daring
minister I have just referred to, who risked unpopularity in the cause of truth. I should think I
have heard fifty sermons on the text 'Almost thou
persuadest me to be a Christian': and of these, not
ten pointed out the inaccuracy of the translation.
One minister, to whom I spoke on the point, said
calmly, 'O, of course it's all wrong, but it makes a
very good text nevertheless': and he defended the
use of Sankey's hymn on the subject. 'After all, we

are dealing with crowds of people who are *almost* Christians.'

This literalism sometimes took very curious forms. When I was about nineteen I happened to fall in with a very charming and intelligent old lady, who must have found it hard to live, even in a two-roomed cottage, on her tiny income of about ten shillings a week. We got, somehow, into conversation on religious topics, and I soon discovered that she knew her Testament almost from end to end. She reminded me of Cowper's weaver, 'pillow and bobbins all her little store', who 'just knew, and knew no more, her Bible true': but that knowledge was a *literal* education, and the way in which she used it was sufficiently startling. By the simple acceptance of every word, she had built up for herself a system of theology which, though perfectly unborrowed and her own, might have come straight out of Calvin's *Institutes*. It was Supralapsarianism *in excelsis*. We were predestined from all eternity to salvation or the opposite; and texts in proof flowed from her lips in a constant stream. One on which she specially relied was 'He calleth his own sheep by name, and leadeth them out'. 'You see', she said, 'they are already *his own* sheep, chosen before the foundation of the world; and they follow him, they can't help it'. In the kindest possible way she hoped that I might be one of the chosen; but if I was not, she hoped that I might have grace to accept my destiny with due submissiveness.

She had been born and brought up in the Church of England, but, finding that the clergyman was impervious to all her arguments, and, as she put it, refused to listen either to John or to Paul, she had ceased to be an Episcopalian and had searched around until she had unearthed a small congregation of Particular Baptists whose views were not in too sharp contradiction to her own. Never have I met a more cheerful person: her happiness shone in her face as she told me of the moment when she first became conscious of her 'election',

> And in that charter read, with sparkling eyes,
> Her title to a mansion in the skies.

That consciousness, she added, she had never, during thirty years, for an instant lost; nor was it possible for her ever to lose it. Once in grace, as the minister told Oliver Cromwell, always in grace.

It was the same with Arminians, though their creed was exactly opposite. Undoubting confidence in the revealed Word of God, though that Word was interpreted altogether differently, produced an indistinguishable result. It was my good fortune to know many people whose lives were so simply beautiful that one would as soon have thought of botanizing on one's mother's grave as of attempting to disturb the faith that gave birth to such serenity and gentleness. 'Leave thou thy sister when she prays.' If I were to draw a picture of such lives, as lived not only in uneducated circles but in some of high culture, I should borrow, without changing a line, the description which Froude gives of the home of the Irish clergyman with whom he lived in 1842, and the sight of whom killed for ever in him his belief in the Tractarian travesty of Evangelicalism. No honest and impartial observer could deny that these people, whatever they lacked, lacked nothing of prime import. If these were not true Christians, then St. Francis and St. Theresa were heathens.

And yet they lacked something, which, if secondary, was not without worth, and weight. Their trust in the Bible was a bibliomania, and could be compared, not unfairly, with a Mohammedan's worship of the Koran. 'Mercy', to quote the words of a favourite poem of the society, Pollok's *Course of Time*, 'had taken down the lamp of Scripture from her everlasting throne, and cast its light upon the dark'. Reading in it certain truths which instantly commended themselves to their minds as answering to their deepest convictions, they extended their trust to every part of the varied literature and even beyond it. Archbishop Ussher was as deeply inspired as St. John; and I have heard 'B.C. 4004' as fiercely defended as any dogma of the Epistle to the Romans. All, even the margins, stood or fell together; two or three dates were like the pillars of the Temple of Gaza—overthrow them, and you destroyed the shrine and yourself with it. The 'days'

in the first chapter of Genesis were periods of
twenty-four hours; the voice was a literal Phēmē
resounding through chaos; the order of Creation
was exactly as described. No one hesitated over the
contradiction between the first chapter and the
next; it was not even perceived to need a harmoniza-
tion. The serpent actually spoke, and presumably
in the Hebrew language—for that language was
unquestionably the dialect of Eden. I have heard
men, otherwise sane, contend that woman has one
more rib than man, as a permanent consequence
of the way in which she came into being. But, as
has been repeatedly noticed, even these chapters,
so jealously conned, were not studied in their own
light. They came clothed in the garb of Milton;
and the story of the Creation and the Fall, which
people fancied they found in Genesis, they had in
fact adopted, at first or second hand, from *Paradise
Lost.* Again and again I have heard incidents
quoted, as if of inspired provenance, which the
quoters thoroughly believed to be biblical, but
which were really Miltonic; and they would be
utterly astonished when, being challenged to find
them in Holy Writ, they failed. This was the more
amazing because, as I have said, they knew their
Bible: but such was the force of tradition that they
unconsciously added to it, and read into it what is
not there. It was, in a fashion, like the influence
which constrained so many scribes, in copying one
Gospel, to intrude into it the well-remembered

phrases of another, bringing *into* the treasury things new and old.

It was out of the question that such persons should attain to a true historical sense. Everything was read through a distorting medium, and Old Testament heroes were regarded as champions of the nineteenth-century Evangelical creed. The shock was thus the greater when, to the educated, there came the impact of geological discovery and Darwin's biological theory. When, after thirty years of comparative impotence, Lyell's crushing assault on the Mosaic chronology forced itself on the notice of these believers, many ceased to believe; others were utterly staggered; yet others treated it as a trial of their faith. Those who know the history of Oxford in Tractarian times will remember how the views of Buckland, though himself a clergyman, struck men like Newman and Pusey as rank blasphemy. The feeling in Low Church circles was the same. And, when the idea of Evolution began to penetrate Church and Chapel, the convulsion was renewed. To a Christian man of science like Philip Gosse it was as if the earth and all the pillars of it were being shaken; men who were not Fellows of the Royal Society looked on with as much horror as Gosse, but without his confidence that the convulsion was but temporary. A few—like Charles Kingsley and others—accepted the new doctrines without fear, and saw in them not a shattering of religion but a buttressing of religion rightly

understood. Many, however, took refuge in stubborn ignorance, and many hoped that vigorous
denunciation might be an effective substitute for
argument.

At about the same time, but more gradually,
came the march of the critical study of the Bible.
I knew ministers who bought *Essays and Reviews* in
order to refute it, but were more or less convinced
by its arguments. Stanley's *Jewish Church*, based on
Ewald, insinuated the poison with a charm which
unadulterated Ewald could never have carried.
At length, even Wellhausen could be seen on ministerial shelves; and Driver, a man of undoubted
piety, slowly undermined the work of his predecessor Pusey. Whispers were heard that tutors at
Methodist colleges were confessing that the Hexa-
teuch was of composite authorship; and very slowly
the conception of a progressive revelation began
to make its way, first into the pulpit and then into
the pew. It became possible to assert that there
were two Isaiahs, and that Daniel was a work of
the time of the Maccabees. Even the agonized
attempts of men like Liddon to stem the tide were
unavailing. Almost imperceptibly, but irresistibly,
it 'won its widening way'; and the vision dawned
on all but the blind that, so far from destroying
faith, this New Learning strengthened it. What,
at first sight, had appeared a retreat, was seen
to be an advance: and, what was of even more
importance, it was seen to be only a preliminary

to further advances. For, though these scholars helped people to a new understanding of religion, they pointed out also that the understanding was far from complete, and that, like Nature herself, Revelation was all but infinite. No study would ever exhaust it; the more knowledge we gained the wider would be the region opened for further search. 'Hills peeped o'er hills, and Alps on Alps arose': and the prospect, so far from filling the explorer with despair, merely spurred him on to further, and more sanguine, exertion. This was the great achievement of that age, the discovery that there were endless possibilities of achievement—and of glorious failure.

CHAPTER VI

WHAT WAS TAUGHT

JOHN WESLEY was that rare combination, an indefatigable evangelist and a theologian. It is no accident that his conversion came about 'while one was reading Luther's Preface to the Epistle to the Romans', or that he was afterwards strongly influenced by the same Reformer's commentary on Galatians. These two letters are perhaps the most specially theological writings in the New Testament, and they may be said to be the foundation-documents both of Lutheranism and of Calvinism. Very shortly after Wesley's conversion, he preached in St. Mary's, Oxford, the famous sermon on Justification by Faith, which he afterwards, of set purpose, placed first in the published collection of his discourses. Justification by Faith, though emphatically practical, is also a theological doctrine of immense theoretical importance.

I should think that scarcely any of Wesley's sermons is without a direct theological reference, and certainly there is none that has not at least an implied theological substratum. Wesley said nothing which he did not think he could fit into the Pauline scheme; and, as I have already said, his

Hymns, unlike many other collections, are 'a body of divinity'. If we knew nothing about him but the volume of 1780, even apart from its famous preface, we should still be able to gather from it his distinguishing tenets, and that though it was designed for public singing and for the private reading of very ordinary people. He believed, on the one hand, that his doctrinal system could be made intelligible to such people, and, on the other, that preaching, whether from the pulpit or by other means, not based on theology, was sounding brass and a tinkling cymbal.

A similar conviction inspired his immediate followers and those who followed *them*. According to their varying capacities, his preachers, who were expected to have studied his first *Fifty-three Sermons* and his *Notes on the New Testament*, endeavoured to put his principles into practice, and to base their own sermons on the doctrines there taught. One or two of these men, like Richard Watson, were fully as profound as Wesley himself; others, like Adam Clarke, made their way to theology through scholarship, but were, none the less, in their special fashion and measure, theologically-minded; and Clarke, indeed, carried his originality so far on one point of dogma as to be held by his colleagues as somewhat heretical. He regarded the phrase 'Eternal Sonship' as a contradiction in terms, and in his *Commentary* did not hesitate to say so. He was answered by Richard Treffry in a small but I think learned book, which was on the shelves of our library, and which—so keen was the theological atmosphere of the time—I was set to read in my earliest teens.

The rank and file of the ministry, of course, were neither Clarkes nor Treffrys; but they preached, with scribal authority, the doctrines they had learned from the standard Methodist writings, and would have scorned to preach what they could not defend as part and parcel of an ordered system. In the main, their sermons might be said to be expositions of 'Articles of Religion', drawn from a Biblical text, 'rightly divided as being the word of truth', but invariably leading to what used to be called the 'application', that is, a stirring appeal, based more or less precariously on the doctrine, to the fears or hopes of the congregation. I have heard some very abstruse and recondite 'articles' ingeniously turned to the practical purpose of gaining conversions or of 'confirming the faith' of converts already made. Not all these 'applications' were as forceful as those of Adam Clarke, which an aged Methodist, who remembered them well, told me were like charges of cavalry; but even the feebler ones of my time were vigorous enough to remind one, both by likeness and by difference, of the 'dancing shape' of which Wordsworth says it 'haunted, startled, and waylaid'. The preparatory exegesis was indeed like the strategy which brings an army to the battlefield, and the final exhortations

were the shock-tactics by which the battle is decided—thunderous, awe-inspiring, and, to some at
least, terrible. The hymn that followed usually
clinched the matter; nor was there then the voluntary, which in later days so often soothed the troubled
breast of the hearers with its meretricious charm.

There remained, in my time, and still remain here
and there, survivors of the ancient days; men whose
sermons show this theological character. I have
often heard discourses denouncing what was then
called Socinianism, confuting Calvinism, or explaining the Arminian conception of Free Will, and yet
somehow, with more or less transitional skill,
working up to the 'application' at the end. Still
more often did I hear warnings against Roman
Catholicism, and definitions of the true Catholicism
which a Methodist might safely hold; Purgatory
was shown to be a fond thing vainly invented, and,
after the obligatory appeal to the hearts and
consciences of the hearers, the appropriate hymn
was given out,

> The saints who die of Christ possessed
> Enter into immediate rest.

A Missionary sermon, not unnaturally, might
disprove the claims of Mohammedanism, and I have
known a minister inform his audience that, in the
lines

> The Unitarian fiend expel,
> And send his doctrines back to hell,

I

the Unitarian meant was the Moslem. But, as a rule, the sermons were not controversial; they laid down, as beyond doubt, the articles of the Methodist creed, and drew from them the maxims appropriate to daily life. A phrase often heard, and one full of significance, was the 'Plan of Salvation'. Man had been created sinless, but with the capacity of sin; he had fallen, and the whole race had been tainted not merely with the capacity of sin, but with sinfulness, which involved an everlasting penalty. The sin, and the penalty, Christ had taken upon himself, and man could obtain remission both of sin and of penalty by accepting, as applied to himself, the 'rigid satisfaction' paid by the blood of Christ. The recognition that Christ shed his blood for *me* was *my* conversion, and meant the consciousness of salvation here and hereafter. To be saved, one must be converted: and the grace of God was always ready to aid the conversion of those willing to receive it; nor was there any limit to the power of that grace. It was free to each, and free to all. 'Thy mercy's beams diffusive as Thy sun's arise.'

There was much in this creed that is to be found in the Confession of Augsburg, which set forth, in 1530, the points at which Lutheranism diverges from Romanism on the one hand and from certain forms of Protestantism on the other. There is the same emphasis on the saving power of 'faith' and the inefficacy of 'works'. As Melanchthon, who drew up that Confession, declared, good works are the *fruit* of faith, not a substitute for it. But Methodism, unlike Lutheranism, insisted on the freedom of man's will, and left the insoluble problem of reconciling omniscience and omnipotence with the existence of evil much as Milton had left it two centuries before. It was a puzzle to amuse the leisure of demons sitting on a hill retired, but not one over which sensible men would waste their time. There were enough difficult questions without it. Antinomianism, which had plagued the Societies eighty years before, had still to be combated, and all sorts of heresies, whether understood or not, had to be denounced.

How often I heard the 'Plan of Salvation' outlined in the pulpit I cannot tell: it was certainly explained so constantly that few indeed in the congregations can have had any excuse for not knowing about it. An American Bishop, over on a visit to England, gave us forty minutes on the familiar theme; and it was astonishing how frequently the attempt was made to compress the whole doctrine into the limits of a single sermon. I should imagine that the case was similar in the French Protestant Church; for I remember reading that, after listening to a trial discourse by a young candidate for the ministry, a wise old pastor said to the preacher, 'My young friend, you have tried to put the complete gospel into your sermon; believe me, no sermon will hold it'. He was right, for even *Paradise Lost* fails to give it in full: and in an oration which had to include 'opening the way to the text', three clearly-marked divisions, and the 'application', it is obvious that there must often have been considerable congestion, even though the listeners were willing to give the speaker fifty minutes or a full hour.

It may well be asked how sermons of this kind should gain a hearing from congregations not trained in theological academics, or how they could be delivered not merely by ordained ministers but by local preachers drawn from the shop, the accountant's desk, or the carpenter's bench. Those who ask this question might be advised to read the history of the Commonwealth times, when a tanner would argue on supralapsarianism and sublapsarianism, and 'divide a hair 'twixt south and southwest side', 'in school-divinity as able as he that hight irrefragable'. It was a matter of interest. As the Scottish congregations, till quite recently, could detect in their ministers the minutest lapse from Calvinistic orthodoxy, or as the populace of Constantinople would argue on subordinationism, because they were interested in such subjects, so the early Methodists talked on imputed righteousness and prevenient grace with the enthusiasm that to-day is reserved for the performances of two football teams. There was a book by Dr. George Smith entitled *A Local Preacher's Manual*, in which, among much sound and sensible everyday advice, the lay-preacher was given the correct views on certain of the most knotty points of divinity; he learnt them, he preached them, and they were discussed afterwards by his hearers. The same author tells elsewhere of a village shopkeeper, one of those small Whiteleys who provided everything from a cart to an ounce of tobacco. He could not read, and kept his accounts by a sort of picture-writing. On one occasion he charged a customer for a cheese, and the bill was disputed. He glanced at his pictorial record. 'Very sorry: it was a grind-stone: I didn't notice the little hole in the middle.' But this man was a keen theological disputant: 'hear him but reason in divinity', and all-admiring you would think he had in his house a Library of the Fathers. He could have given Thomas Aquinas something to worry about.

One of my early memories—of course from a much later date than the *floreat* of this remarkable tradesman—is of a minister who had strayed, like Adam Clarke but without Clarke's prestige, into heretical by-paths. Cautiously and tentatively, he had ventured to adumbrate a theory as to the peccability of Christ's nature. His caution, how-ever, was vain. He was detected by one of the poorest of his hearers, and promptly reported to his superintendent, who, I suppose, dealt efficiently with the delinquency; for the minister, perhaps quoting *sotto voce* the words of a once-familiar hymn,

> Watched by the world's malignant eye,

took care never to offend again. How many people are there to-day capable of noticing such a heresy, or of troubling about it when noticed? Many years later, I happened to be hearing an eminent Church of England clergyman, who, *mirabile dictu*, chose as his subject the doctrine of the Trinity. He had not gone far when I perceived that he was explaining the mystery on the lines of Sabellius, an undoubted heretic, who had been excommunicated so far back as A.D. 261. But, though every word of the preacher ran counter to the Athanasian Creed, I could discover no signs of embarrassment in the congregation, nor did I hear that any appeal was afterwards made to the Bishop of the diocese. Had that sermon been preached in a Yorkshire village chapel in 1840, the Chairman of the District would have heard of it. I fear also that there was the same decay of theological acumen in Nonconformist circles, and on points of more general interest than so obscure a subject as Sabellianism. For, at about the time when the heretical clergyman was discoursing, I heard a sermon on the effect of Baptism on Original Sin, from a Dissenting pulpit, which was certainly tinged with Romanism, and which, whether orthodox or not, would, fifty years before, have been critically canvassed. At the end, there was a hymn, and then the Benediction. There followed the voluntary, which, if there were any flames of indignation, effectually quenched them.

Why this keen interest prevailed, and why it died out, who can tell? The wind bloweth where it listeth, and a subject which at one time is not thought dull simply because nobody thinks of it at all, attracts wide attention, and drives out another which it had seemed as if men must discuss or die: and then, for no apparent reason, the attraction ceases in its turn, yielding place to new. Certain it is that the strictly theological sermon gradually declined; the ministers sensed that it was no longer holding the congregations, and made their appeals in other ways. Some of the abler pastors, in some of the more highly educated towns, adopted the purely expository style. They were studying the newer critical commentaries, and, with the requisite modifications, gave the results of their studies on the Sundays. They read Lightfoot, and it is a significant fact that Hort said of Lightfoot on Galatians, 'There is everything in it except theology': a saying which, a few years before, would have meant 'There's nothing in it worth having'. But the new preachers preferred to have it so. Others, who were of an artistic turn, contrived to blend religion with painting or music, and showed that there was no inconsistency between sanctity and beauty. Historical sermons became common.

And—to the scandal of old-fashioned people—the sermon began to busy itself with topics of the day; some of the more popular preachers took up a novel and analysed it from the religious point of view, or availed themselves of the vogue of a scientific treatise to secure that interest which theology could no longer command. I have heard discourses on Kidd's *Social Evolution*, though I cannot recall the texts on to which they were tacked; and I have heard others of which the Academy Exhibition supplied the main substance. As for Holman Hunt's *Light of the World*, I suppose that it suggested several thousand pulpit-homilies in its time.

Carlyle died in 1881—many scores of obituary services, and myriads of repetitions of the phrase 'the Sage of Chelsea'.[1] Darwin died in 1882; how far was Evolution consistent with Christianity? The quater-centenary of Luther came in 1883; there were hundreds of sermons on his life, but few, so far as I could ascertain, on his characteristic dogmas. Browning and Bright died in 1889—there were half-hour biographies of both. But perhaps the *annus mirabilis* was 1892, in which Tennyson, full of years and glory, was gathered to Shakespeare, Milton, and Virgil. Here was a mingling of poetry and piety. A slight touch of theology as one glanced at 'In Memoriam'; five minutes on the

---

[1] Later, I heard various discourses on Carlyle. The one I recall most clearly dwelt on the thoroughness and diligence with which he digested his authorities: an example which youth might do well to follow.

Arthurian pattern as exemplified by the Prince
Consort; twenty minutes of eulogy of a Laureate-
ship in which, as in the reign of his predecessor,
'nothing base' was uttered; a fervent peroration,
and room was made for the choir and 'Crossing the
Bar'. But where was the 'application' with its
cavalry-charge? and where was the dogmatic
background of yester-year?

There were notions, hardly to be dignified with
the name of doctrines, which the attendant at chapel
in the 'forties' would inevitably hear expounded.
The most commonly proclaimed of these was that
of special providences; and it would be hard to
exaggerate the effect of this idea on the lives and
habits of the people. The laws of Nature were
constantly being suspended for the benefit of the
good or for the punishment of the bad. Wesley's
Journal is full of narratives of these Providences;
a shower of rain or a sudden cessation of a shower,
a stumble of his horse, an illness or a recovery, everything, in fact, marked that he was being watched
by some invisible messenger from on high. Miracles
were all round him; an earthquake was effected
directly by the Almighty; a Catholic girl's blindness
was a punishment for reading the Missal. Such
beliefs, though it would be easy to parallel them
in the lives of High Churchmen and Catholics,
have given occasion to the enemy to blaspheme, and
have been ignorantly ridiculed as if peculiar to
Evangelicals. They lasted long after Wesley's

time; and the reader will remember how they roused the fury of Sydney Smith. There is, I think, little harm in them when they lead men to think *themselves* preserved from danger; but they are unmitigatedly mischievous when they are turned against others. 'Judgements' ought to be exterminated, and indeed, since the story of the Tower of Siloam was told, ought never to have appeared in the Christian Church. But it is scarcely too much to say that not a week passed without a solemn report of a judgement on a sinner, and assuredly not a number of the *Arminian Magazine* appeared without ten or a dozen guaranteed stories of the kind: how a bee stung the 'unruly member' of a blasphemer, how a clergyman fell dead at the card-table, how a man, swearing and ranting at a cock-fight, was struck dead, how a storm of thunder and lightning drenched and terrified a man going on an evil errand. No one can understand early Methodism who does not realize that the Societies were saturated with these ideas, and that the people were living in the atmosphere of monastic miracle as described by the Venerable Bede. It is this revival of 'the grossest superstition', in the enlightened eighteenth century, that fretted such a writer as Lecky, willing as he was to do justice to the movement.

It was an unconscionable time in dying. In my youth I heard many such stories, and I have known those who doubted their significance to be branded as infidels. God, said the believers, does 'interfere' by 'strange dispensations' to pass open judgement on sinners: and if, like Asaph, you wonder that these dispensations seem so capricious, you are presumptuously censuring the Almighty. I recall many sermons on Byron, in which the poet's misfortunes were traced to his wickedness; and at least one on Shelley, in which an old minister declared his early death was the vengeance of heaven on his atheism. A young hearer was severely rebuked for suggesting that a similar sermon might have been preached on the prince who was 'taken away from the evil to come'. How, in fact, all this could be reconciled with the teaching of certain texts by people who believed in the verbal inspiration of Scripture is difficult to understand.

There is, however, just this to say in favour of such sermons that at any rate they said *something*: and, during the first half of the nineteenth century, this was a comparatively rare virtue. 'The great object of modern sermons', said Sydney Smith, 'is to hazard nothing; their characteristic is decent debility, which alike guards their authors from ludicrous errors, and precludes them from striking beauties.' In reading them 'we must wade through many a barren page, in which the weary Christian can descry nothing all around him but a dreary expanse of trite sentiments and languid words'. The old Methodists did not disguise their thoughts, and, if they sometimes thought wrong, and expressed their ideas in wild and whirling words,

their hearers at any rate were in no doubt as to
their meaning. And this was specially the case with
what we may call the Terror-sermons, those in
which future punishment was dwelt upon with the
frenzy, if not with the poetry, of Dante. Here the
Arminian was at one with the Calvinist and the
Catholic. An unlimited supply of death-bed stories
was at the disposal of the speakers, and was drawn
on to its capacity. The eternity of the anguish was
emphasized equally with its intensity; and the
sinner, if he could not be persuaded into heaven
had to be frightened into it. In certain cases the
effect was disastrous: some lives were made miser-
able with fear. In others, I think, it was the reverse
of what was intended; people revolted against such
a picture of God, and, like John Stuart Mill and
others, rejected *in toto* a religion of which this
doctrine was asserted to be an essential part. But
of this subject enough has been said by others. The
dogma was gradually whittled away, and the
ministers sought other means of attracting their
hearers into the Church. I have not heard one of
the old fashion for many years: and I do not believe
that, whatever be the causes of the decline in church
attendance, the cessation of such sermons is one
of them.

I think, however, that despite the immense
importance of the sermon in the Methodist services,
and despite also the less palpable influence of the
hymns with their theological background, the main

teaching work was done by the ministers in their pastoral capacity : and a good visiting minister, like a family doctor, conveyed a vast amount of quiet instruction to his people, the effect of which, if seen at all, was seen only after many days. I have heard advice sought and given as to books to be read, and books to be avoided ; stores of information have been released on history and biography, especially, of course, concerning Methodist heroes. I have been present when George Smith's *History of Methodism*, or D'Aubigné's *History of the Reformation*, was recommended to eager inquirers, and I have more than once been the errand-boy conveying the precious volumes from the ministerial library to a family which had no other means of procuring them. The instruction sometimes took the form of a dissertation on the illimitable range of knowledge, and on the wisdom of Socrates as shown by his proud confession, 'One thing I know, that I know nothing'. I recall vividly the look on the face of a 'parishioner' as he talked with a minister whom he regarded, with some justice, as a very learned man. 'Why don't you publish books yourself?' he asked, when a dozen books by others had been passed in rapid review. 'Because', was the answer, 'I know nothing which the world does not know already'— a reason which it is to be wished, many writers had borne in mind. The talk then turned on the awed humility of the greatest scholars as they con- templated the little they knew and compared it with

the illimitable field of what remained to be known.
He who can teach this, has taught the most valuable
of all lessons.

When the minister found a well-informed layman,
it was a liberal education for the family to listen to
the talk as it ranged easily over all sorts of themes—
mainly, as might be expected, the ecclesiastical.
I have heard men who could tell first-hand anecdotes of the great Scottish Disruption of 1843; who
could describe Dr. Chalmers as they had seen him
in the pulpit, or Candlish as they had watched him
in debate; and who could appraise these great
heroes with discrimination, comparing their styles
with those of Dr. Bunting, Robert Newton, or
Dr. Beaumont, the contemporary glories of Methodism. Or the conversation might take a literary turn;
and here, though the views might be limited, the
criticism was keen. I have heard discussions of
Milton, Wordsworth, Byron—admiration shot with
horror—Burns, and perhaps oftener than any,
Cowper: and, whatever names came up, there
would be ample quotation. I think the academic
scholar would have been astonished to find how
ready and well-equipped these amateurs were.
I remember well a wholesale grocer whose leisure
was devoted to history, and on whose shelves were
the well-thumbed works of our greatest historians.
At his table I listened to an account of the quarrel
between Freeman and Froude, which was then
raging with a fury like that of the fire of London.

After the meal, I happened to notice a work on the Geography of Herodotus, jostling a translation of the History. 'You'll never find a more delightful book than that', said the gentleman—for such he was; and taking down the book he chatted pleasantly on the adventures of that garrulous old traveller, with a freedom and ease which any scholar might envy.

Not infrequently the advice asked and given was on practical affairs; for, if the minister had earned confidence and respect, that advice was valued. The son of a man of my acquaintance had been disrespectful to his mother. Before deciding what to do, the father consulted his minister. Those were the days when the problems of adolescence had not been studied, and too often such offences were dealt with in accordance with the good old rule, the simple plan of bodily chastisement, and parents were usually as vigorous in following Solomon's maxims as schoolmasters themselves. But the minister was of another cast of mind. Drawing not on theory only, but on a long experience, he shewed his friend that such a method might easily lead to permanent antagonism between child and parents, and, with some little difficulty, persuaded him to give a trial to the law of kindness. Finally, the lad was brought in, and a few sympathetic words from the minister produced the desired effect. Without the slightest apparent compulsion the boy went direct to his mother and made a full apology; a complete reconciliation followed, and what might have been a family tragedy had a happy ending. What is more, there was thenceforward in that little household an almost unchequered harmony; and the respect in which that minister was already held deepened into a lasting and unshakable reverence.

I could tell more stories of the kind, and probably there are many more which have never been told.

CHAPTER VII

POLITICS

FROM THE THIRTIES we may fairly date the real interest of the British people in politics. It has been said that everyone was a politician in the time of the Stuarts; but that interest, keen as it was, died down after a time, and, in the absence of newspapers, could not be kept up continuously. The tremendous excitement of the Reform Bill agitation was perhaps no greater than that aroused by the attempted arrest of the Five Members, or, forty years later, by the Exclusion Bill; but circumstances allowed its effects to be more lasting. It gave the vote to many thousands of men who had not had it before, and who wished to use it, even if only as a mere toy. It disappointed many thousands more, who had been led to expect the millennium, and had got little or nothing. Satisfaction and discontent were alike expressed in the daily paper or the weekly sheet, and the papers fanned the feelings to which they owed their existence. They were expensive, but they could be passed from hand to hand, and the expense could be shared. The *Times*, for instance, cost sevenpence or fivepence, and therefore sold only thirty thousand copies at the height of its

influence, but every copy was read by scores of
people, and a well-known painting shows the
eagerness with which they waited their turn and
the envy and impatience with which they watched
the man in possession. There were other papers,
legal and illegal, all over the country, spreading
news and defending opinions such as their readers
wanted. Tories, Conservatives, Whigs, Liberals,
Radicals, Chartists, and even a few Socialists were
all reading, talking, voting, demanding the vote,
or gloomily foreboding horrible evils should the
vote be given. Men were interested even in what
was said in Parliament, and the speeches of their
members were known to them. There were the
Reform Act in 1832, the Chartist troubles in the
'forties', the upheavals of 1848, the Crimean scandals
in 1855, the fear of invasion in 1859, and hundreds
of other events to stir the thoughts of the people.
In Palmerston's last years there was quiet, but only
because people were willing to 'let the old horse
pull the coach for the present'. As soon as the old
horse should be gone, they would rush forward
again; and when it *was* gone, they did indeed rush
forward.

There was still a lively belief in Parliament, along
with what now appears an almost infantile trust in
the power of publicity to influence it. Charles
Reade, for example, thought that 'it was never too
late to mend' if he could only induce the Press to
print a letter on the evils that required mending;

and men of less eminence held the idea equally firmly. Tell the world what was wrong, and Parliament, like the Round Table of old, would ride abroad redressing it. It was widely maintained that, if other countries adopted a free Press and Parliamentary institutions on the British model, all would be well; and many countries did adopt them—for a time. A few jests, not usually unfriendly, were made on the 'Houses of Palaver', and a few influential men, like Carlyle and his disciples Ruskin and Froude, raised their voices against a system based on talk, crying out loudly but vaguely for men of action instead of chatterers. Even Macaulay, a most successful Parliamentarian himself, admitted that ability to orate was not the same as ability to act or rule; but he pointed out that after all a device which gave us Pitt or Fox was better than one which gave us a 'Steenie' Buckingham or a Bute. Carlyle, on the other hand, never showed how his men of action were to be discovered; and people, reading him with avidity, were constantly asking that question, and were as constantly disappointed. The heroes he eulogized were not always admirable, and the means they had employed to gain power were often flagitious to the last degree. He was also in the inconsistent position of being a ceaseless talker himself, and his thirty-seven volumes in laudation of silence did not seem to practise what they preached. Thus he might pipe, but the people, though they listened, did not dance. To become a Member of Parliament was still a high honour, and a man who wished to do good in the world tried either to become a member himself or to interest a member in his schemes. It was thus that the economists induced Ricardo, much against his personal inclinations, to enter the House, and remain there for a few months. Advocates of 'Temperance' tried, sometimes with success, to elect Teetotal candidates. Men like Thackeray and Trollope, whose studies of certain conditions had given them ideas as to possible improvement, stood for Parliament but failed to secure election. 'Tom Duncombe', a voice crying in the wilderness, expounded to heedless benches the point of view of the Chartists, and Michael Sadler, member for Leeds during all too short a time, pointed out the absolute inapplicability of the doctrine of free competition to the case of starving labour when it strove with prosperous employers.

Upon all this, Nonconformity, as time went on and as it gradually became used to the new conditions, began to exert a very powerful influence, constantly increasing till the Great War altered everything. Dissenters found they could make and unmake ministries. They put Gladstone in power in 1868, and, in disgust at the Education Act of 1870, threw him out—to repent at leisure—in 1874. So active were they, especially in the great towns, that they were constantly accused by their opponents of thinking more of politics than of religion. Their ministers, it was said, preached Liberalism rather than Christianity, while their congregations, para-doxically enough, introduced too much religion into politics. At any rate they affected politics pro-foundly. Even before they made their great step forward in 1832, they had done much by the support they gave to Wilberforce in his campaign against slavery; and the 'Clapham Sect', strongly Church of England as it was, owed an immense debt to its Evangelical friends outside the Establishment. After the Reform Act, many Nonconformists entered Parliament. A Northern manufacturer, indeed, was often Nonconformist by upbringing and tradi-tion, and did not disguise the fact. At first, indeed, he was scarcely at home among the squires and younger sons of peers who still formed the vast majority of the Lower House, and his Dissent was as strange to them as his Yorkshire accent. Even those who sought his aid could not help showing a certain condescension, not always very tactful. Everybody has heard of Lord Fitzwilliam's unlucky quotation. Unable to get enough money for the restoration of York Minster from Church people, he turned to the Nonconformists, saying, in the words of Virgil's Juno, 'Flectere si neque superos, Acheronta movebo', which may be roughly trans-lated, 'If heaven won't help me, I'll apply to hell': and in Parliament, for several years, the same atti-tude might often have been observed. But gradually the prejudice, within the walls of the House of

Commons, that most tolerant of assemblies, broke down. Even in the heyday of Palmerston's glory, and in the very height of Bright's unpopularity, there was wide indignation when the old worldling called his Quaker antagonist 'the honourable and reverend gentleman': and later, when Bright had recovered his influence, his Quakerism no more stood against him than Lloyd George's Baptist connexions stood against him in 1917.

By far the best represented 'sect' in the country, for the fifty years with which I am concerned, was the Unitarian; it was but slowly that the others found a place proportionate to their numbers and power in the country at large. The Methodists, as I have already shown, hung back for a considerable time, and the ministry remained on the whole Tory while the laity were growing steadily more Radical. With the great Chartist movement of the 'forties', as with the earlier Reform movement of 1815 to 1832, the body, as represented, perhaps badly, by its leaders, showed little sympathy. James Heald, the first Methodist Member of Parliament, was, if I remember rightly, a Tory, and was congratulated as such by the President of the Conference of 1847 which followed his election. But his Toryism, like that of Lord Shaftesbury, was of the philanthropic kind; he is still remembered, after nearly a hundred years, as the founder of the Stockport Infirmary. From that time forward, Methodism took more and more of its proper place in the great council of the nation, and, as it became more and more Liberal, contributed its share, with the other Nonconformist bodies, to 'peace, retrenchment, and reform'.

Nonconformity had here one great advantage, due to its predominantly democratic constitution. On the average, the Nonconformist, ministerial or lay, has vastly more opportunities of practising the arts of speech, and not least of extempore speech, than the Anglican. A Methodist, for instance, is always speaking, at Quarterly Meetings, in the Sunday School, as a Local Preacher, in debating societies, and he has constantly to get up and address an audience on the spur of the moment. At prayer meetings he has perhaps almost too much liberty of prophesying. Compare the *ordinary* Methodist minister, on a sudden emergency, with his clerical brother. The one, accustomed to giving three or four more or less impromptu sermons, and five or six addresses, every week, will be easy and fluent; the other, whose prayers have been dictated to him by Cranmer, and whose ten-minute discourses have been perhaps read from a manuscript, will be halting and uncomfortable: and, though the man of genius will overcome these disadvantages, the ordinary clergyman will remain ordinary. Similarly, compare the average Town-councillor of Methodist upbringing with one who, in the Church, has been more of a listener than of a speaker. There is *no* comparison. The speech of the

men betrays the religious surroundings of their
youth: one is almost too fluent, the other is a
stammerer whose hums and haws fill up a quarter
of his time.[1]

It was in democratic Churches like these that
Chamberlain learned his easy and telling oratory,
his power of debate, and his quickness of retort.
Here Bright gradually perfected his unmatched
simple English style, his unforced pathos, and his
invective; here, in later days, Lloyd George acquired
his strange gift of catching inspiration equally from
the sympathy and from the antagonism of his
audience. I well remember how, when hearing
Henry Fowler, afterwards Lord Wolverhampton,
and noticing the force, the directness, and the
passion of his eloquence, I was at once able to trace
it to its origin in a Methodist church-room, where,
perhaps, under the eye of his father, he had made
his first essays at public speaking. Elsewhere I
have told how a venerable Methodist ex-President,
called on at a moment's notice to propose a vote of
thanks to Mr. Balfour, gave that halting and hesitat-
ing speaker a lesson in the art of extemporary
oratory. In a little address of four or five minutes,
with beginning, middle, and end, with every word
exactly the right one, and a touch of humour to
enliven it, he showed a perfection to which
Mr. Balfour was totally unaccustomed, and which

[1] It has recently been shown how the Chartist leaders borrowed their
organization from Methodism, with its class-meetings, circuits, and the
rest.

he afterwards acknowledged to have been un-equalled in his experience save by Gladstone and Bright. But the old gentleman was not speaking for the first time. He had gained this skill by daily exercise, and by the careful study of the best English writers, begun in his teens and carried on for fifty years.

In a country ruled by talkers and regulated by that most remarkable of all British products, the chairman, the advantages of such an education were soon manifest. A speaker thus trained could dominate a Corporation, and, so soon as he had breathed the atmosphere of the House of Commons, could make himself influential there. The list of distinguished politicians of Nonconformist origin—though many tried to forget the rock whence they were hewn[1]—is an astonishingly long one: and the list of famous barristers is equally impressive.

But the real strength was, after all, less in Parliament itself than in those who made the Parliaments. The Liberal Party, on the whole, between 1830 and

---

[1] Some, like Samuel Waddy and William Willis, never forgot or disguised it. Everybody knows how Waddy continued to preach even after he became a Judge: and the story of his adventure with Frank Lockwood is still remembered. Lockwood, in a spirit of mockery, went to hear him. Waddy, seeing him at the back of the chapel, announced at the end of the central hymn, 'And now my friend Sir Frank Lockwood will continue the service'. Sir Frank, eloquent as he was in the presence of juries, felt unequal to facing a Methodist congregation, and incontinently fled.

As an example of the kind of training in oratory to which I have referred, I might mention a case I witnessed myself at the age of ten. At the school chapel, the minister who was expected to preach failed to appear, and the Head Master called on the senior boy to take his place. The lad, not yet nineteen, acquitted himself admirably, giving us a sermon of twenty minutes without faltering or ever pausing to choose a word. He afterwards became a well-known Yorkshire Congregational minister,

1880, held the power: and it probably would not have been in power for a single year without the Nonconformist vote. Even when the Tories were in office, they had to listen, however little they liked it, to the Nonconformist voice: Sir James Graham, for example, had to withdraw his Education Bill in the face of Dissenting opposition, and that though the Government of which he was a member was one of the strongest ever known. Sometimes, it is true, the force was exerted for unworthy causes, and was guided by narrow views. Thus, in 1844, Sir Robert Peel was seriously embarrassed by the antagonism of the Methodists and Evangelical Churchmen to the Dissenters' Chapels Bill. Many of the old Presbyterian congregations had gradually and insensibly become Unitarian; and an agitation, led by people who ought to have known better, was started to deprive these congregations, in consequence of this change, of their chapels and endowments. Most fortunately, Peel was strong enough to resist the attack; but what I am here concerned to note is that the attack was dangerous, though unjustifiable. In the following year he was subjected to another, still more violent, onslaught, when he proposed to increase the endowment of the Roman Catholic college at Maynooth. Here again, though the main body of the assailants was Tory, inspired by the usual Tory inability to understand Irish desires, yet much aid was lent by Nonconformists, whose fear of Catholicism blinded them to their illiberality and unfairness. The fury was portentous. To quote once again the oft-quoted words of Macaulay, 'the Orangeman raised his war-whoop; Exeter Hall set up its bray; Mr. Macneile shuddered to see more costly cheer than ever provided for the priests of Baal at the table of the Queen; and the Protestant Operatives of Dublin called for impeachments in exceedingly bad English'. By the help of the Whigs, Peel was able to pass his Bill, and to escape a defeat which, if he had depended solely on his own supporters, would have been certain and crushing. But once more, though unsuccessful, Nonconformity was able to shew its power. Macaulay's words were remembered against him: Exeter Hall took its revenge, and a considerable part in Macaulay's defeat at Edinburgh at the next General Election was played by those who could not forget his contemptuous treatment of that home of Evangelical eloquence.

There were other movements of a more reputable kind, in which Nonconformists bore their part. In the great Free Trade campaign the work of the Quaker Bright will never be forgotten; but, at the time, it was doubtful whether either Bright or Cobden was more effective on the platform than the Unitarian minister, W. J. Fox, who was also distinguished as a journalist, and especially for the articles he published under the name of Publicola. Fox was chosen by Dickens to write the first leader in the *Daily News*, then as now (*News Chronicle*) an

uncompromisingly Liberal paper; and the tone
Fox set has been maintained ever since.

In the Free Trade battle, as in other struggles,
motives were doubtless mixed. Free Trade in corn
was obviously to the advantage of the Northern
manufacturers, as the real worth of the wages they
paid would be increased by cheapening food; and
it was only human that these men should see the
moral merits of their material interests. They were
indeed accused by their enemies of adopting the
cause as a counter-attack on the agriculturalists
who were supporting the Ten Hours Bill and the
other restrictions on the licence of the masters to do
what they would with their own. One may admit
the charge in many cases; but the movement as a
whole was, beyond doubt, a noble one, inspired by
a genuine philanthropy; and it is mere cynicism to
deny that those who sacrificed time, money, and
health in the cause were, in the main, acting for the
love of their fellow creatures and in the fear of God.
There was human infirmity even in Clarkson,
Sharp, and Wilberforce; but that does not diminish
the glory of those who, in the face of obloquy,
continual disappointment, the defection of friends,
and the loss of fortune, at last put an end to slavery
and the slave-trade. In their own way, those who
aided Bright and Cobden might be compared with
the helpers of Clarkson.

Every deduction being made, in fact, I think that
the effect of Nonconformist work in politics is

something to be proud of. In the Temperance movement there was unquestionably fanaticism; but none who know the state of things in 1840, and compare it with the state of things to-day, will deny that the good far outweighed the harm, or that those who actually saw the horrible evils may be excused for even some excess of zeal. It is easy for those who, like the gentlemen of England, sit at home at ease, away from the danger and the fury, to criticize the spirit of the fighters in the battle; but it is pretty certain that no battle was ever won without fanaticism of some kind. If a soldier, instead of fighting, spends his time in reflecting that the enemy may have something to say for himself after all, he is not likely to be victorious: and the Teetotallers were then in deadly conflict with a fearful enemy. That they should not be over-particular in their words or methods was inevitable.

The same thing may be said, *mutatis mutandis*, about many other causes which Nonconformists supported. We now know, for instance, that there was much to be said for the South in the American Civil War; indeed, if it had been a matter solely of constitutional legality, it would have been extremely hard to decide which party was in the right. Not so long before, when conditions were different, certain Northern States had threatened to secede from that very Union which now they passionately proclaimed to be one and indivisible. The South was only doing in 1860 what New York had been

about to do in 1812 : and yet New York was fighting
to prevent the South from doing it. But Nonconformity in England, and the Northern workers
generally, did not trouble about legal niceties.
They went to the heart of the problem, and
recognized that while the South was nominally
claiming only the right of secession, it would never
have claimed that right but for its dependence on
slavery. Hence, while almost the whole of the upper
classes supported the South, and went on blindly
ignoring facts till the very last moment; while the
Government was involving itself more and more
inextricably in a tangle, the influence of Nonconformity was used in the opposite direction. When
things had come to such a pass that a proposal was
actually made to reconcile North and South in
a joint war against England, it was as well that a
strong body of opinion was there to prevent the
folly from going too far: and here again we need
not be surprised if that opinion failed to express
itself on every occasion with the calm detachment
of an historian writing years later and in surroundings far removed from the din of battle. Men may
have been too undiscriminating in accepting the
point of view of *Uncle Tom's Cabin* and the Abolitionists generally, and they may have failed to see that
many men among the Confederates were actuated
by as high motives as their own; but in the main
they saw true, and it was well for the country that
they did so.

In a similar spirit, some years later, they threw themselves eagerly into Gladstone's campaign against Disraeli's anti-Russian policy. Disraeli may not have been as deliberately wicked as they thought him; he had not, like Faust, sold himself to the devil; but they were convinced that his proceedings were not only unwise but actually immoral. He was protecting a murderer against an avenger, and threatening war against a Christian Power on behalf of one which was not only not Christian but the very negation of all that Christianity stands for. They therefore supported Gladstone with all their strength; and Disraeli must have known that, if he actually did go to war, he would not have a unanimous country behind him. How far this knowledge influenced his plans is hard to say; he was not the man to reveal his motives; but the fact remains that, despite the 'Jingo' frenzy, the secret pressure of Queen Victoria, and the dangers into which his own course had led him, he did avoid war, and brought back in his own grandiloquent phrase, 'Peace with Honour'. That the people whom he and his followers were never tired of ridiculing and denouncing as sanctimonious hypocrites had *something* to do with the result is more than likely. And that they were, on the whole, right is, I suppose, now pretty generally admitted. Lord Salisbury is not the only Tory to confess that his party, through these troubled years, had put their money on the wrong horse.

It was about this time that we began to hear the
mutterings of an opinion which later expressed
itself in the sarcastic phrase 'the Nonconformist
Conscience'—a modern rendering of Burns's 'Unco
guid' or rigidly righteous. Men were annoyed at
what seemed to them an assumption of superior
sanctity, as if Nonconformity was saying, 'Doubtless
we are the people, and religion will die with us': as
if the 'people' were Christians and their opponents
at best worldlings. It is not pleasant, when you have
adopted a certain opinion or a certain policy, on
what seem to you good grounds, to be told that the
other side has a monopoly of virtue, and to hear, if
only in imagination, 'Stand aside, for I am holier
than thou'. The complaint was that whereas most
political questions are merely matters of expediency,
on which good men may be allowed to differ, the
Nonconformist conscience claimed to decide all on
religious grounds, and either refused to allow its
opponents the possession of a conscience at all, or
declared that what they had was seared with a hot
iron. Especially were Conservatives irritated when
Dissenting pastors began to take an open share in
party-warfare, and to use their pulpits as if they had
been hustings. The Methodists, in general, were
free from this latter crime; but they were, as private
individuals, equally prone to what was called the
Pharisaic habit of treating their friends as Israelites
and their enemies, at best, as proselytes of the
gate.

There was certainly something in these accusations. Nonconformists, at times, certainly did try to make up for their social disabilities in this world by booking seats in celestial mansions; and pulpiteers sometimes, in their zeal for noble causes, were inclined to call other people's eye evil and their own good. And when a scandal arose, they were too much inclined to a self-righteous attitude. The demand, for instance, which they made that every public man should be what is known as 'moral' meant simply that he should not be found out. Carried to its logical conclusion, it would have meant that Wellington should have been cashiered long before Waterloo, and that half our Prime Ministers should have been relegated to private life. At best, or rather at worst, it would have crowded our Cabinets and our public services with hypocrites, and our political leaders would have kept their places, as the Ashleys did in Commonwealth times, by squeaking more loudly than other bagpipe-players in the national orchestra. On more than one occasion this kind of inquisition did untold harm, and was duly at once ridiculed and utilized in countries which had been accustomed to Metternichs, Bismarcks, or Napoleons.

Nevertheless, the question is not to be decided off-hand. Where some political point arises in which a moral issue is really involved, it is not easy to say that a minister ought not to speak, or that an important class of society ought not to express

L

an opinion based on ethics. On such a question as that of the Contagious Diseases Acts, to which Josephine Butler devoted her life, it seems to me that it was not merely the right but the duty, alike of the pulpit and of the pew, to speak with no uncertain voice. The difficulty is to decide in those borderland cases in which morals shade off into 'commodity'; a recent instance, in which a Bishop of the Church of England ventured into this dubious region, and in which he was loudly applauded by some for his courage and as loudly denounced by others for his meddling, shows how impossible it is to satisfy all sorts and conditions of men. Doubtless, in the past, many people, as conscientious as the Bishop, made mistakes of judgement, and were betrayed into imprudence. But many, by speaking out plainly at opportune moments, and by reminding the world that England is, at least in theory, a Christian country, did a service which cannot be denied. Even if there is much in politics which cannot be determined on religious grounds, a certain honourable tone, or even that homage which vice pays to virtue, is by no means undesirable in our statesmanship; and nothing tends to maintain this tone so well as the sense that the statesmen are being watched by men of virtue and honour, who will not fear to speak when they think that the public standard is being lowered. It is one of the best things in our history that Gladstone, Grey, and other statesmen did not fear to appeal to this

national conscience, and that the national conscience rarely failed to respond. A converse instance
is the universal indignation aroused by the scandals
which led to the legislation on the 'Plimsoll Line'.
Here the conscience of the people was deeply and
instantaneously stirred, and the Government yielded
at once. No one, I think, could in this case have
rightly objected to a clergyman or minister who
should, in a different spirit from Chaucer's Pardoner,
have preached on the text, 'Radix malorum est
cupiditas'. Plimsoll, in his indignation, might
express himself in unparliamentary language, and
be censured by the Speaker; but it was right and
just that he should receive the compensating
approval of religious men.

If on questions of home-politics there was this
difference of opinion, on foreign affairs it might be
expected that the differences would appear in
exaggerated form. At times, it is true, this was in
some degree the case. There is no doubt, to take
one instance, that John Bright's opposition to the
Crimean War not merely was directed against the
unwisdom of the whole policy which brought it on,
but was inspired also by general religious motives,
and by the Quaker attitude, also emphatically
religious, towards war. The opposition, again, to
Palmerston's high-handed action with regard to
China, on the Lorcha 'Arrow' incident of 1857, was
led by truly religious men, regardless of the certain
loss of their popularity, and willingly facing the

likelihood, which soon turned into actuality, of their defeat at the next election. As we have seen, the Civil War in America, and the Disraelian anti-Russian policy, were viewed by men in accordance with their religious views and feelings. But there were intense antagonisms, due in some cases to these very feelings and the sympathies they naturally engendered. A Churchman, as a rule, had Tory friends, lived in Tory surroundings, and had Tory inclinations. Thus, though there was nothing to be said against his personal piety, he would inevitably tend to see the best side of Tory policy. There were good men who supported Peel's sugar-duties, though they involved indirect assistance to the slave-owners of the South in America. There were good men who passionately defended the Crimean War; and there is a remarkable contrast between the denunciations of so admirable a man as Bright and the eulogies of the not less devout Dean Merivale, which can be read in his *Life*.[1] On the Irish question, which, though always with us, assumed special importance between the 'sixties' and the 'nineties', many Nonconformists were led to oppose Irish aspirations by their natural sympathy with the Protestants of the North, while many

[1] This difficulty is amusingly illustrated by the perplexity of a dear old aunt of mine, one of the best women I ever knew. Two friends of hers differed on politics. 'What am I to do?' she asked. 'They are both, I know, good men, but one says one thing and the other another. How *am* I to decide?' The reader may recall what Hurrell Froude said to his younger brother Anthony: 'When Newman and Keble disagree, you may think for yourself.' Till then, he was to let them do his thinking for him.

Churchmen, whose tendencies might have been
expected, because of their 'Catholic' leanings, to be
the other way, were drawn into an alliance with
these extreme Dissenters by their Tory and Imperial-
istic sentiments. Stranger bedfellows, on either side,
have rarely been seen than these.

But the most marked feature, to one looking back,
in the religious politicians of those days, was the
conspicuous absence of an abhorrence of war as
such. Apart from the Quakers, while there was a
hatred of aggressive war, very few Christians,
clerical or lay, Anglican or Dissenting, asked more
of a war than that it should be capable of being
dubbed, in the good old phrase, 'just and necessary'.
That even one to which these two adjectives might
be attached could need defence, seemed to occur to
nobody. There was then no 'Dick Sheppard'; and
an undergraduate who should, even as a paradoxical
jest, have proposed a motion against fighting for
King and Country would have been thrown into the
river to the satisfaction of all the pulpits in the land.
Nor did one hear many censures even of reprisals,
though Marmont had proclaimed their uselessness
and though the Lord had said 'Vengeance is mine'.
In the passions of the Indian Mutiny, there were
men, and humane religious men, who rejoiced
when captured mutineers were blown from guns,
who excused the atrocities of Hodson, and who
blamed the 'clemency' of Canning. Whereas Lee
and Joseph Johnston said they thought the slavery

question ought to have been settled in a better way than by war, men of prayer praised the bloodshed. On the Franco-German conflict of 1870, the point discussed was which of the two combatants was to blame, and not whether Christ, who said 'Resist not evil', might not have blamed even the attacked party whichever it was. No Cadoux, as far as I remember, had yet discussed, with any thoroughness, the attitude of the early Christians to the army; but I think that men who had cast a casual glance on that portion of history were inclined to sympathize with those of the heathen who complained that the Christians would claim all the benefits the Roman Empire conferred on them, and never raise a finger to defend it. Many went further, and turned their eyes on the glories of war, 'just' or 'unjust': it was a school of virtue, a training in unselfishness, and a bulwark of patriotism.

I am not here prejudging the question as to the rightness or wrongness of out-and-out pacificism. I leave it where Ruskin left it when he confessed that he could not speak of war without contradicting himself. What I wish to say is that it is a question which Christians *must* discuss, and which *must* embarrass them. But it was not, except in the rarest cases, discussed at all in the Victorian age. I have heard men pray, 'Scatter thou the people that delight in war', and have seen them gloating, a little later, over an Archibald Forbes's description of a battle. One of my very earliest memories is of

coming down to breakfast in a house of very
religious people with whom I was staying, and of
noticing that the family seemed particularly happy.
It appeared that the French had won a victory,
which must have been their solitary success, at
Coulmiers, by which von der Tann was driven
from Orleans. I was too young to know who the
French were, or what a battle was; but I vividly
recall how the children listened to the joyous tones
of the father as he read out the details of the combat.
There was not one word expressing horror: there
was the short sentence, 'Thank God': for by that
time the sympathy of our people was swaying from
the side of Germany to that of France. There was
still a belief in the God of battles; and though
Coventry Patmore had already sent his sarcastic
doggerel[1] on the German Te Deums to the *Times*,
it was not thought absurd to praise the Deity for a
victory of which you yourself approved. At the
beginning of the war, the Germans, who were
regarded as sound Protestant Christians, had the
right to pour out thanksgivings, for they were the
instruments of the Almighty in chastising the
irreligion and frivolity of Gaul. As the British
feelings changed, Providence was assumed to change
with them. It was on the side of the *weaker*
battalions.

[1] It may be now forgotten:
> Now God be praised, my dear Augusta,
> We've had another awful buster:
> Ten thousand Frenchmen sent below,
> Praise God from whom all blessings flow.

I think many people to-day will hold that, whether Canon Sheppard was right or wrong, it is as well that men like him should exist: for his point of view is one that ought to be put. When Alexandria was bombarded in 1882, John Bright resigned from the Government—a solitary remonstrant. A Christian minister I knew remarked that the bombardment was a good thing—it taught the barbarians not to despise the British Navy. To-day there would, in such a case, be a dozen resignations, thousands of remonstrants, and not a dozen voices daring to say that the thing was anything at best but a terrible necessity. Here, at any rate, one can discern a great advance in the last fifty years. Whether the next fifty will show advance or retrogression, who can say?

CHAPTER VIII

CONCLUSION

DEAN MILMAN, in his *History of Latin Christianity*, after describing the terrible state of the Church in the early centuries, the Councils with their quarrels, their confusions, and even their murders, the furious anathemas, the persecutions of heretics by the orthodox, of the orthodox by heretics, and of heathen by both, observes wisely that if we were to fix our gaze solely on these horrors we should be inclined to think the religion of Christ a very poor substitute for the beliefs it displaced. But he adds that it is the errors and the crimes that are blazoned in history. To understand the permanence of Christianity one has to remind oneself constantly that beneath the turbulent surface there was a quiet life of peace, charity, and faith of which we gain knowledge only incidentally and occasionally. The real saints were not the Cyrils or even the Leos, but the people of whom we scarcely hear.

In the times of which I have been speaking there were no such tumults as those which Milman had to relate. There were indeed quarrels, disruptions and upheavals, the effects of which have scarcely even yet died away. There were libels and slanders, and much uncharitableness, befitting rather ancient Athens than modern England, and the worship of the war-god rather than the worship of Jesus. But, compared with what happened in Constantinople or in Alexandria, this might be called mild; nor did two rival Church prelates ever lead armies against each other, and seek peace by bloodshed, as they did in Rome. Nevertheless, the words of Milman are, in their measure, applicable to the Victorian age as to the Theodosian. I have had to tell of many unpleasant things, and of many mistakes both in act and in opinion. One might easily fancy, therefore, that religion has had but little influence in restraining human passions or in mitigating human troubles. But one would be wrong: for here again, despite the pryings of Press-men and the research of historians, true religion hides itself, and blushes to find fame. A murder attracts a thousand times the notice given to a kindness, and a word in season provides less 'copy' than a scandalous invective. And here the historian, to a certain extent, is like the reporter. He deals not with mute inglorious dwellers in the hamlet, but with those whose virtues or whose crimes have been shown on a conspicuous stage.

Thus when, in these few pages, I have dwelt on the gross errors of religious men in politics, on their support of bad causes, on the excessive violence with which they had supported a just cause, on their insensibility to cruelty and oppression, or on their perhaps be invidious to try to answer. But I have a shrewd suspicion that the historians of the next century may be inclined to judge us with a little more severity than that with which we judge ourselves, and that they may find something to censure in the very complacency with which we have blamed our predecessors. Why this sense of superiority? they may say. It is by no means certain that the improvements brought about in the next half-century will be comparable with those achieved by our grandfathers in the fifty years between 1830 and 1880; and such advances as may be made will have been made possible by those earlier advances, for which, it cannot be denied, religion, applied to social life, was mainly responsible.

Read the newspapers of the thirties, and note the ferocity with which the editor of the *Morning Chronicle* assailed the 'filthy *Times*', and the equal vigour with which the 'Thunderer' retorted. Turn then to the news columns, and, accustomed as you may be to the sordidness of to-day, look at the descriptions of public hangings, remembering that nearly all these executions were for trifling offences, for which to-day a week's imprisonment or even a binding-over might be a sufficient penalty. Or take down J. L. and B. Hammond's *Village Labourer*, and see in what a state of misery that poor creature lived, and how savagely he was repressed if he made the slightest effort to mend his condition. Read Dickens, deduct all you like for his exaggerations, and compare his pictures with those which a man of similar genius—if such there be—would draw to-day. There is enough room for improvement still, God knows. But that there has been an immense step forward is equally certain. And, if you impartially inquire to whom we owe this advance, you will be compelled to own that it is in no small measure due to men and women, often mistaken, sometimes precipitate, but religious, and, while steadily pursuing the service of man, faithfully and honestly worshipping God.

PRINTED BY WESTERN PRINTING SERVICES LTD., BRISTOL